PAINLESS
Vocabulary

Michael Greenberg, M.A.
Illustrated by Tracy Hohn

Second Edition

To my colleagues

All inquiries should be addressed to:
Barron's Educational Series, Inc.
250 Wireless Boulevard
Hauppauge, New York 11788
www.barronseduc.com

ISBN: 978-0-7641-4714-2

Library of Congress Control Number: 2010049946

Library of Congress Cataloging-in-Publication Data
Greenberg, Michael, 1951–
  Painless vocabulary / Michael Greenberg ; illustrated
by Tracy Hohn—2nd ed.
    p. cm.
  Includes index.
  ISBN: 978-0-7641-4714-2
  1. Vocabulary—Problems, exercises, etc.
  PE1449.G665   2011
  428.1—dc22   2010049946

Printed in the United States of America
10 9 8 7 6 5 4 3 2

CONTENTS

CONTENTS

INTRODUCTION

Words Don't Hurt: How to Use This Book

There's an ad on the radio that cracks me up. It claims there are fifty-five essential words—the keys to success—and if you know them and can use them, you can change your life. I have no idea what those words could be! I'm thinking along the lines of "I love you" and "Will you marry me?" and "I think I deserve a raise," but most of us probably know those words already.

The point is that there's no easy road to developing a better vocabulary. If you're highly motivated—if you care very much about language and grades and SAT scores—you may as well know that you've got a lot of work ahead of you.

This book can help.

The book consists of twenty chapters. Each will introduce fifteen new words to you, for a total of 300 words. (Along the way you will encounter other words related to these, so your vocabulary will grow by more than the featured 300.)

How can anyone guess which words you most need to know? That—despite the advertisement mentioned above—would be impossible. The words in this book are the kind of words that middle school and high school teachers incorrectly assume that students already know. They have been taken from established middle school and high school vocabulary lists, which are often based on words chosen from well-known literature, books like John Steinbeck's *The Pearl* and Harper Lee's *To Kill a Mockingbird*. Chances are, you have seen many of these words already; they will be familiar to you. Perhaps you have already come across them in your readings or on television. They are not too hard, nor too easy. Some of these words may have specialized meanings, but this book will emphasize the everyday ones.

Each chapter begins with an essay that includes in context all fifteen list words (in red type). After that, the words will be introduced to you five at a time. These introductions will provide you with italicized synonyms for many of the words. You will find a host of different Brain Ticklers that will determine whether you have acquired some mastery of these words. A sidebar (a related article) entitled Major Mistake Territory will alert you to certain pitfalls and problems involving the list words in particular and vocabulary acquisition in general.

Other sidebars will assist you in developing the kinds of skills that will help you boost your vocabulary on your own. One sidebar, for example, will tell you how new words enter the English language. Another will help you use a thesaurus.

Another section, which appears toward the end of each chapter, is called On Your Own. Here you will have a chance to use all or some of the vocabulary list words within the context of your own language. At the very end of each chapter, a section called The Last Word will offer some parting thoughts on some aspect of the chapter's contents.

The answers to the Brain Ticklers will appear at the end of every chapter.

You have purchased this book because you are motivated to improve your vocabulary. Using this book is an excellent beginning. It will add more than 300 useful words to your vocabulary, and it will provide you with some skills and strategies to permit your vocabulary to grow way beyond that.

Now let's get started.

CHAPTER ONE

Dinosaur Man
Words in Context

When Luke was barely two years old, he developed an extraordinary awareness of dinosaurs. This awareness was unusual not only for the ardent nature of his interest, but also because of the boy's age.

It all began in Luke's preschool. His teachers introduced the children to a set of dinosaur models, which Luke promptly scrutinized. On the drive home from school, he regaled his mother with tales of triceratops and tyrannosaurus and velociraptor. She decided to stop at the nearby bookstore to procure a few dinosaur picture books he might enjoy. Enjoy? He simply devoured them. As his mother read to him, Luke pondered the miracle of creatures so different from those he knew.

It soon became obvious that Luke's love of dinosaurs would endure. Anything with a dinosaur pattern elicited from Luke expressions of sheer glee, so nearly every gift from friends or family catered to this taste. Before long, representations of dinosaurs adorned his bed sheets and pillowcases, his shower curtain, his bath mat, and even the walls of his room.

When Luke's teachers completed the dinosaur unit and moved on to Native Americans, Luke's passion for the former did not abate. His parents arranged a trip to various zoos and museums. They visited New York's Museum of Natural History, whose dinosaur display enthralled the future paleontologist.

Meet Words 1 through 5!

1. Extraordinary sometimes means *supernatural*, but in this case its usual meaning, *beyond ordinary*, applies. Luke's interest in dinosaurs is rather extraordinary for two reasons: his age and the degree of his interest.

2. I feel ardent about thin-crust pizza and really great books and the first cool days of autumn. But you probably feel *passionate* about something else, right? (By the way, ardent comes from the Latin *ardere*, which means "to burn." If you feel ardent or passionate about something, you practically burn for it.)

3. A good writer will scrutinize a first draft in order to locate any careless errors she has made. Only by *examining* her work very closely can she hope to produce first-rate writing. That's how closely Luke examined those dinosaur models.

4. To regale is to *delight*, to *entertain*. Sportscaster Tim McCarver knows so much about baseball that he's sure to regale his listeners with his knowledge of the game.

5. You can procure or *obtain* a quart of milk from the super-market or the corner deli. If you're looking to procure a high-paying job, you'll have to look harder.

BRAIN TICKLER
Set #1

Match 'Em Up: Synonyms

Synonyms are words that mean almost the same thing. For example, "select" and "choose" are synonyms. There are three reasons for you to learn synonyms. First, identifying a synonym can help you understand a particular word. Second, you can pick up additional words to improve your vocabulary. For example, when you learn that "challenging" and "formidable" mean about the same thing, you have learned another word. The third reason is that words have shades of meaning. You might learn that "difficulty" and "hardship" are considered synonyms, but that "hardship" is a stronger word, one that suggests difficulty that is very hard to bear. So . . . select the word closest in meaning.

1. ____ extraordinary: a. plain b. daily c. astonishing d. pleasant

2. ____ ardent: a. enthusiastic b. clear c. involved d. occupied

3. ____ scrutinize: a. enjoy b. read c. arrange d. inspect

4. ____ regale: a. bore b. confuse c. entertain d. destroy

5. ____ procure: a. seal b. obtain c. rescue d. convince

(Answers are on page 13.)

Major Mistake Territory!

When selecting synonyms and antonyms, you must keep in mind parts of speech. If the list word is an adjective, you must select as its synonym or antonym another adjective. For example, "scrutinize" is a verb. You can choose as its synonym "examine," another verb, but you cannot choose "examination," a noun.

Meet Words 6 through 10!

6. Because of my ardent desire for them, I devour great books and thin-crust pizza. "Devour" means to *consume* or *eat greedily*.

7. Ponder comes from the Latin *ponderare*, which means "to weigh." When you ponder the steps you must take in order to ace your science exam, you weigh this subject in your mind. You give it the time it deserves.

8. When the Greek gods made his life miserable, the hero Odysseus had no choice but to endure, to *keep going*, to carry on, to "hang in there." Sometimes that's all we can do when trouble comes our way.

9. To elicit is to *bring forth* or *draw out*. A good teacher will ask questions in a way that will elicit superior responses from his or her students.

10. Sheer has two common meanings. It can mean *complete*, as in the case of Luke's sheer glee, or it can mean *very thin* or *transparent*, in the sense of sheer curtains or a sheer fabric.

BRAIN TICKLER
Set #2

Words in Context

Words in context. If you don't know the exact meaning of a word, you won't necessarily run to a dictionary. You're more likely to use the words and sentences around it to figure out the word's meaning. (See the sidebar later in this chapter.) Choose the list word (devour, ponder, endure, elicit, sheer) that best completes each sentence.

1. Kindness is contagious! One act of kindness may _____ another.

2. When Henry saw his perfect test score, he boasted of his _____ brilliance.

3. Nowadays we hardly have to _____ muscle pain; anyone can easily purchase over-the-counter painkillers.

4. Theresa hadn't eaten in hours, and she couldn't wait to _____ the meal placed before her.

5. Maya liked to think about infinity, a concept she could _____ for hours.

(Answers are on page 13.)

Meet Words 11 to 15!

11. You may have used a caterer to provide food for your party, but the verb cater means simply to *provide* whatever is needed or desired. If your parents cater to your every need, then you'll never learn to do things for yourself.

12. Students' work should adorn the bulletin boards of a class-room. That makes sense, right? What else would you use to *decorate* a place of such intellectual accomplishment?

13. Former means *previous* or *first*. Would you like a brief homework assignment or a long one? Most students would prefer the former (not the latter).

14. Until this storm abates, I think I'll just pull over to the side of the road. Only when the rain *subsides* or *stops* completely will it be safe to drive.

15. To enthrall is to place under a spell, or simply to *captivate*. (Originally, the word "thrall" meant a "slave." It's easy to see how one might be enthralled by a spectacular view or a wonderful performance . . . or by the skeleton of a huge dinosaur!)

BRAIN TICKLER
Set #3

Word Forms

Here's a paragraph that includes list words 11 to 15 (cater, adorn, former, abates, enthrall). Insert the correct form of each word in the proper blank.

Boxing is a violent sport, a fact that (1) _____ many of the sport's fans. When you see a fighter's shorts (2) _____ with a skull-and-crossbones logo, you know that some of the sport's participants are only too eager to (3) _____ to their fans' thirst for blood. Many retired fighters, including (4) _____ heavyweight champ Muhammad Ali, suffer from the excessive blows they have absorbed in the ring. Until the public's love of violence (5) _____, we can count on more violence in the ring and more injuries to the sport's practitioners.

(Answers are on page 13.)

WORDS IN CONTEXT

Each chapter in this book begins with a brief essay. The main purpose of this essay is to introduce the words that you will learn within the chapter. You probably have seen many of these words before, and you may already have a pretty good idea of their meanings. The introductory essay will give you an even better idea if you're capable of finding the meanings of words in context.

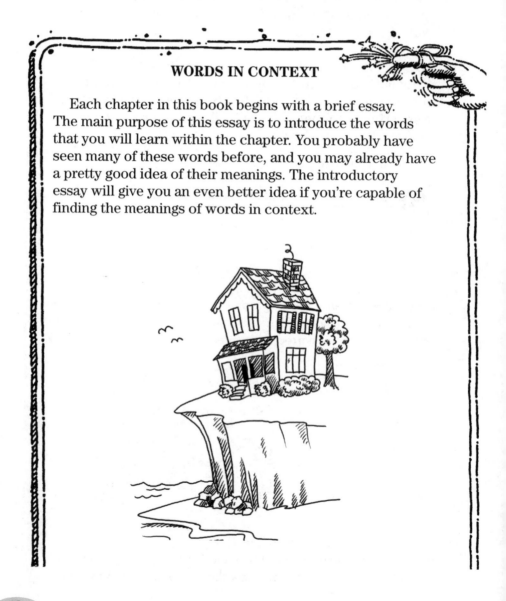

In a general sense, the word "context" refers to a whole situation, or a set of meaningful circumstances. For example, if you were to see a photograph of a small wood-paneled house, you might use words like "cute" or "pretty" or "ordinary" to describe it. However, if you were to view that same house in its natural context—say, on a cliff, overlooking an ocean beach—you'd have a much better understanding of what that house is really about.

In a more specific sense—having to do with language—"context" refers to the words and sentences surrounding a particular word or phrase. It is this context that gives that word or phrase its most accurate meaning. (Sometimes you will hear someone complain that his words have been taken "out of context," because their meaning is not considered in light of what was said before or after.)

If a writer uses a word the reader is unlikely to know, he may include contextual information that practically defines the word. Here are a couple of examples:

- Mrs. Simmons began the meal by serving a bowl of vichyssoise, a cold soup made from potatoes and onions.
- On the wall of the den, Frank mounted a very rare derringer, a small handgun first used in the nineteenth century.

Chances are you did not know the meanings of "vichyssoise" and "derringer," but that's all right, because the writer of these sentences anticipated that and gave them to you.

While writers may often provide the definitions of specialized terms, a reader sometimes must work a little harder in using the context to find the meaning of everyday vocabulary.

This is what readers usually do. As they are reading, they don't stop to use the dictionary every time they come across a word whose meaning they don't know. Instead, they use the context to find the meanings of unfamiliar words.

To do so, a reader must look elsewhere in the sentence and in the paragraph to obtain a good sense of the word's meaning. Let's take another look at a paragraph from the introductory essay:

It all began in Luke's preschool. His teachers introduced the children to a set of dinosaur models, which Luke promptly scrutinized. On the drive home from school, he regaled his mother with tales of triceratops and tyrannosaurus and velociraptor. She decided to stop at the nearby bookstore to procure a few dinosaur picture books he might enjoy. Enjoy? He simply devoured them.

As a reader you have probably come across the word "scrutinized," but if you were asked the meaning of the word in isolation—without any words surrounding it—you might not know. However, the first section of the essay gives you a pretty good idea of its meaning. The reader says to himself, "I know that Luke is really wild about dinosaurs. What would he do if his teachers put in his hands a set of dinosaurs?" He would check them out really closely, which is what "scrutinized" means.

The reader is probably familiar with the behavior of young children. Luke is thrilled to have learned just a little about dinosaurs. On the ride home from school, he would share this excitement with his mother. The reader can probably conclude that "regale" means "entertain."

"Procure" is easy. Luke's mom is stopping at the bookstore to "get" or "purchase" a couple of books that will satisfy her son's new interest.

The reader might not know the meaning of "devour," a word usually used in reference to foods. But it's obvious that Luke more than enjoyed the books his mom had procured for him: he simply gulped them down.

BRAIN TICKLER
Set #4

Words in Context

Choose the correct list word to complete the sentence. Look for context clues! The list words for this chapter are: extraordinary, ardent, scrutinize, regale, procure, devour, ponder, endure, elicit, sheer, cater, adorn, former, abate, enthrall.

1. The Brandts look forward all year to their tree-trimming party, where everyone gets a chance to select a trinket to _____ the tree.

2. The new chief executive knew he'd have a hard time trying to equal the _____ leader in terms of popularity, effectiveness, and reputation.

3. When his parents showed their son his first bicycle, an expression of _____ delight appeared on the boy's face.

4. As the campfire burned, the scoutmaster _____ the boys with a couple of amusing ghost stories.

5. The principal, hoping to _____ a confession, told the student in great detail all the convincing evidence he had gathered.

6. The restaurant owner knew what his customers liked, and he made a pile of money because he was smart enough to _____ to their tastes.

7. After Philip had been caught cheating, his teacher sent him to detention and encouraged him to use his time there to _____ the foolishness of his ways.

8. Before you sign that contract, you had better _____ each and every word.

9. Because Romeo had so _____ly confessed his true affections, Juliet could find little reason to hide hers.

10. The New York Yankees began the season in _____ fashion by playing a pair of games in—of all places—Tokyo!

11. Even though you earned only a B on the third-quarter report card, now is not the time to _____ your efforts; with a solid fourth quarter, you can still earn an A in this class.

12. Yitzhak Perlman's violin solo _____ the audience, who could only wonder how so much lovely sound could emerge from so small an instrument.

13. After having fasted for an entire day, Bill _____ the first meal that was placed before him.

14. When TV first appeared on the scene, some people wondered whether this new invention would _____, but now, many years later, TV is more popular than ever.

15. Terri had so much fun using her friend's Play Station that she was eager to _____ one of her own.

(Answers are on page 13.)

ON YOUR OWN

The introductory essay describes a young child's fascination with dinosaurs. Can you remember a time in your life when you were similarly fascinated? Maybe your fascination wasn't with dinosaurs. Maybe you focused your energy on a new toy or a video game or your first cell phone or a sport or maybe even a subject in school.

Write a good body paragraph (that is, one with a strong topic sentence, several supporting sentences, and a strong clincher sentence to wrap it up) about that fascination. Include at least five list words from this chapter.

THE LAST WORD

We use so many words to describe intensity. For example, abate means to lessen in intensity. But a word like devour means something more than simply "to eat," right? It means "to eat with much intensity."

Which other list words reflect intensity?

BRAIN TICKLERS—THE ANSWERS

Set #1, page 4

1. c
2. a
3. d
4. c
5. b

Set #2, page 6

1. elicit
2. sheer
3. endure
4. devour
5. ponder

Set #3, page 7

1. enthralls
2. adorned
3. cater
4. former
5. abates

Set #4, page 11

1. adorn
2. former
3. sheer
4. regaled
5. elicit
6. cater
7. ponder
8. scrutinize
9. ardently
10. extraordinary
11. abate
12. enthralled
13. devoured
14. endure
15. procure

The Last Word, page 13

ardent, scrutinize, regale, enthrall, extraordinary, ponder

CHAPTER TWO

In Your Face!
Word Forms

Here is a scenario you have seen many times.

A basketball player streaks so far ahead of the field that opposing players have abandoned any hope of catching him. He begins his leap, soars toward the basket, and throws one down with such vengeance that you would think he has just managed to free all his loved ones from a hopeless hostage situation. Moments later, as soon as he descends to earth, he clenches his fists, opens his mouth wide, and screams to the fans with unimaginable joy.

His behavior suggests a unique occurrence, but that is not the case. Fans will not have to wait ten minutes to see this—or some other player—celebrate a nearly identical play.

Americans have grown accustomed to poor sportsman-ship from their sports heroes. On the hard courts, on the clay courts, in the end zones, and on the bases, athletes gloat about their great and minor victories, and they whine when hard luck arrives. To a veteran sports fan, it is a dreary event.

The real problem, however, is that the kids are paying very close attention.

Across the country, children—some very young—have learned to argue with umpires, shout insults at the other team, brag about their accomplishments, and ignore those of their competitors. Coaches lament their players' bad manners and wonder how they can begin to instill the right attitude in chil-dren who just don't want to hear it. (What makes the situation even worse is the behavior of some parents. These poor role models openly root for their children, "boo" those on the other team, and argue loudly with each other, the coaches, and the umpires.)

Kid sports are supposed to be fun, but fun becomes impossible when one player is determined that his or her fun must come at another's expense. An important part of sports is learning how to act properly toward everyone else involved in the game.

But how can we expect children to be humble when on every sports network arrogance is on display?

Meet Words 16 to 20!

16. If a basketball player streaks ahead of the field, players will abandon, or *give up*, any hope of catching him. If you were to find a puppy abandoned on the side of the road, you'd probably want to find a home for the poor creature.

17. To soar is to *fly high*. Basketball players do it, and so do airplanes. In another sense, a student's grades can soar. For that matter, so can the printed word.

18. You can probably detect in vengeance the root of the word "revenge." (Both words come from the Latin *vindicare*.) Vengeance is the desire to pay someone back for some hurt—to give a hurt for a hurt. Sometimes we say that an act has been performed "with a vengeance," which means that it has been done with great intensity and purpose.

19. To descend is *go down* or *come down* or *fall* from a higher place. A bird may descend from its perch high in a tree. Sometimes we use the word to refer to family histories: Sharon descends from a family of music lovers.

20. To clench is to *grip* or *hold* very tightly. In his famous poem "The Eagle," Tennyson pictured the claws of that bird clenching the very edge of a cliff.

BRAIN TICKLER
Set #5

Descriptions Inferred from Comments

Choose the vocabulary word from these list words (abandoned, soar, vengeance, descends, clench) that describes the person who would make the comment.

1. _____ "I'll get even with her if it's the last thing I ever do!"

2. _____ "This money is mine! It's mine! And I'll never let it out of my hands!"

3. _____ "Has anybody seen my teacher? Has anybody seen anyone in my class?"

4. _____ "Wait for me down there. I'll be down in just a minute."

5. _____ "I got the highest grade in the class! I studied for hours and hours, and it paid off!"

(Answers are on page 28.)

Meet Words 21 to 25!

21. If a thing is unique, it's *one of a kind*. For example, if a coin is unique, it is bound to be very valuable.

22. If you are accustomed to a particular experience, then you are *used to* it. You can probably recognize in this word the root word "custom," which refers to a particular practice.

23. An athlete who gloats is not displaying good sportsmanship. Such an athlete is happy with his accomplishment . . . maybe a little too happy.

24. Do you become annoyed when you hear someone whine? It's easy to dislike someone who keeps complaining and complaining in an annoying tone of voice.

25. A veteran is someone who is experienced. A veteran teacher (it can be used as an adjective) is someone who has been teaching for a number of years. Sometimes "veteran" has a very specific meaning, referring to someone who has served in the military.

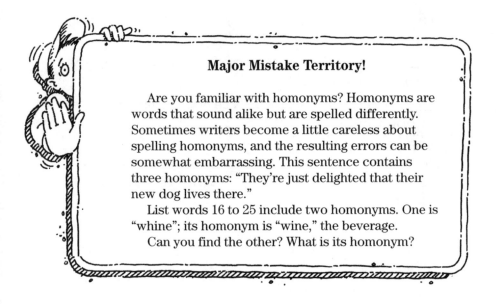

Major Mistake Territory!

Are you familiar with homonyms? Homonyms are words that sound alike but are spelled differently. Sometimes writers become a little careless about spelling homonyms, and the resulting errors can be somewhat embarrassing. This sentence contains three homonyms: "They're just delighted that their new dog lives there."

List words 16 to 25 include two homonyms. One is "whine"; its homonym is "wine," the beverage.

Can you find the other? What is its homonym?

BRAIN TICKLER
Set #6

Extremes

Think about words that suggest extremes. Would you rather eat a *tasty* burger or a *delicious* one? Would you rather go to the beach on a *pleasant* day or on a *spectacular* one? Each of the following sentences contains a list word and one paired with it. Circle the word that suggests an extreme.

1. She has one green eye and one blue one, which is pretty unusual/unique, if you ask me.

2. Ms. Walter is so fed up with/accustomed to students who ask the same question another student has just asked that she assigns detention to these repeat questioners.

3. "I know you did great on the test," Wally said, "but I don't see why you have to mention/gloat over the fact that your score was three points higher than mine."

4. "We have no choice today but to complete our household chores. I wish you would just get started without all the annoying complaining/whining."

5. The school was looking for a capable/veteran teacher, instead of someone fresh out of college.

(Answers are on page 28.)

Meet Words 26 to 30!

26. Dreary means *dull* or *dismal,* and it can describe the weather or one's mood or just about any experience that you wish would soon end.

27. To lament something is to *regret* it deeply, but sometimes it can be a noun—an expression of deep regret or mourning. Coaches lament the shortage of players who demonstrate proper respect for their opponents.

28. Good teachers instill in their students a love of learning. In other words, they *inspire* them to want to learn more and more. Coaches who want to instill in their players a sound approach to sportsmanship have a tough task ahead, because the players often pay closer attention to the gloating role models they see on television.

29. When we say a person is humble, we mean that individual is *modest.* He doesn't think too highly of himself or his own accomplishments. When we speak of a person's humble home, we mean there is nothing fancy about it. It may even be the residence of a poor person. Humble can also be used as a verb, in which case it means to bring someone down. In 2004 the Red Sox certainly humbled the Yankees when they came back from 0–3 to defeat them in the post-season.

30. If we think of the noun form of humble—humility—then its opposite is arrogance. When an athlete displays arrogance, she's showing that she thinks she's better than the other players. When a politician or businessman displays arrogance, he is showing that he doesn't believe the rules that apply to others apply to him.

BRAIN TICKLER
Set #7

Synonyms

Synonyms are words that mean almost the same thing. Select the word that is closest in meaning to the list word. Remember that if you don't know the meaning of one of the choices, you can use the process of elimination. In other words, if you can rule out the other choices, then the remaining one—even if you're not certain of its meaning—might be correct.

1. _____ dreary
   a. honest   b. stimulating   c. depressing   d. cute

2. _____ lament
   a. grieve   b. memorize   c. confuse   d. predict

3. _____ instill
   a. impart   b. realize   c. learn   d. practice

4. _____ humble
   a. luxurious   b. unremarkable   c. complicated   d. special

5. _____ arrogance
   a. sweetness   b. sense of humor   c. intelligence   d. superiority

(Answers are on page 28.)

WORD FORMS

Take a look at the word "unique." You know that this word is an adjective. It can describe a noun or a pronoun: "The waterways of Venice make for unique travel throughout the city."

But you know also that you can change "unique" to an adverb by adding "-ly": "After a good meal, a bowl of ice cream is uniquely satisfying."

The advantage of recognizing word forms is that you easily double and triple the number of words you're learning. Here's another example. The list word "abandon" is a verb, but "abandoning" can either be a verb ("The child mistakenly thought his mother was abandoning him") or a noun ("Abandoning a pet is a thoughtless way to get rid of an animal you don't want").

Keep this in mind as you attempt the following task.

The word bank below includes alternate forms of some of the list words. See if you can insert them in the correct blanks.

Word Bank: arrogant, whiner, descendent, vengeful, customary

1. Stop complaining about the long car ride! Nobody likes a _____.

2. Sarah learned that she was a _____ of a famous Civil War general.

3. In Barcelona it is _____ to say "hello" and "good-bye," but the citizens don't care so much about "please" and "thank you."

4. Ted suggested that Luis lose his _____ attitude and simply learn to forgive and forget.

5. Tennis star Bjorn Borg was never accused of being _____; he always treated his opponents politely.

(Answers are on page 28.)

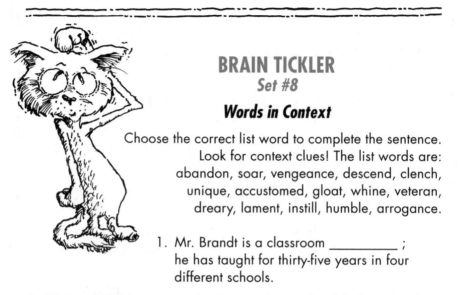

BRAIN TICKLER
Set #8

Words in Context

Choose the correct list word to complete the sentence.
Look for context clues! The list words are:
abandon, soar, vengeance, descend, clench,
unique, accustomed, gloat, whine, veteran,
dreary, lament, instill, humble, arrogance.

1. Mr. Brandt is a classroom _____ ;
   he has taught for thirty-five years in four
   different schools.

2. Terry read 200 pages of this horribly boring book before deciding
   to _____ it and choose another.

3. You must realize that if you _____ over your excellent test
   score, you will offend those who did not do as well.

4. When a world-class golfer clubs that ball just right, it's fun to watch
   it _____ above the fairway.

5. The painter's work was so breathtakingly brilliant that it served to
   _____ in lesser painters a desire to reach a certain level.

6. Weather-wise, it's just a(n) _____ kind of day, yet I don't mind
   sitting by the window and watching the rain come down.

7. Only a professional model could _____ a staircase with the
   grace of a ballerina.

8. Our hosts prepared _____ food for the barbecue: franks,
   burgers, fries, lemonade . . . nothing very fancy.

9. When ten-year-old James received his very first paycheck for his
   newspaper delivery route, he _____ the money tightly and
   raised his hands in celebration.

10. After running a marathon, Julia was exhausted and hungry, yet she attacked her post-race meal with a(n) _____.

11. "Please pass the maple syrup," Rebecca said. "I am _____ to having lots of syrup on my pancakes."

12. The jeweler examined the ring very carefully. Finally he exclaimed, "I have never seen one like it. I think it is _____."

13. In an unpleasant display of _____, Richard said he knew he would win the spelling bee and he was surprised his competitors hung around so long.

14. Some of the old-time sportswriters _____ the passing of an earlier era, when professional athletes and reporters socialized together and befriended each other.

15. Finally Tim's father let him have it: "You can watch your show in fifteen minutes, when your brother's is done. I can't stand it when you _____."

(Answers are on page 28.)

ON YOUR OWN

Pretend you are the coach of a middle school team. Using at least five words from this chapter, create five rules of sportsmanship that you would want your players to follow.

1. _____

2. _____

3. _____

4. _____

5. _____

THE LAST WORD

Instill comes from the Latin word *instillare*, which means "to put in drop by drop." Earlier you read that good teachers tend to instill a love of learning in their students. You may be interested to note that this inspirational process—this instilling of a love of learning—doesn't happen all at once. Inspiration happens drop by drop. It takes time. For this reason, anything that's instilled tends to remain. That's true, too, of a love of language: it comes to you drop by drop, but once you have it, it's yours forever.

BRAIN TICKLERS—THE ANSWERS

Set #5, page 19

1. vengeance
2. clench
3. abandon
4. descend
5. soar

Set #6, page 21

1. unique
2. fed up with
3. gloat
4. whining
5. veteran

Set #7, page 23

1. c
2. a
3. a
4. b
5. d

Word Forms, page 24

1. whiner
2. descendent
3. customary
4. vengeful
5. arrogant

Set #8, page 26

1. veteran
2. abandon
3. gloat
4. soar
5. instill
6. dreary
7. descend
8. humble
9. clenched
10. vengeance
11. accustomed
12. unique
13. arrogance
14. lament
15. whine

CHAPTER THREE

The Writing Process– The Long, Slow Road to Nearly Perfect

Read, Read, and Read Some More

According to Greek mythology, Zeus, the king of all the gods, suffered from a terrible headache. He summoned his son, Hephaestus, the god of the forge, and Zeus begged him to offer any relief he possibly could. Hephaestus lifted his ax and brought it down squarely on his father's head. Out sprung Athena, the goddess of wisdom, fully grown and entirely perfect.

This sudden birth of perfection is not a good model for the writing process, but too many student writers think it is.

When students are given an assignment, they do what students typically do—they procrastinate! After wasting the required amount of time with whatever distractions are available, they eventually find a "quiet" spot to work (it's just an iPod that won't bother anyone else). Forty-five minutes later, a piece of writing emerges. The following day, this sheet of paper finds itself on the teacher's desk.

Several days later, when the paper is returned, the student is dismayed to learn that the grade is not as high as she had hoped. She complains that the demanding teacher is too critical, that this cold, aloof person has never warmed to her personality, and that she loathes the subject anyway.

The problem is that students are not willing to work hard enough on writing. The two essential steps that students often overlook are planning and revising. Planning can take lots of different forms. One needn't spend hours pondering an assignment, and a complex outline is not the only end product, but it's safe to say that the more time one spends planning, the less time one will need for the other steps.

Most students think that revision is simply a matter of using the spell-check feature of a word processing program. Others believe in going a little further—eye-scanning the piece for words left out and homonym errors. Both are mistaken. Revision means taking a good hard look at what's been written. It means that the writer must examine the logic and the fullness of her ideas, and she must determine whether her piece is convincing.

Seldom does a student-writer create a first-rate piece without taking these steps.

Meet Words 31 to 35!

31. To summon is to *call* or *send for*. You may have heard of a legal document called a summons (a noun), which requires someone to appear before a court.

32. Typically is an adverb, and it means just about the same as *normally* or *usually*. Do students typically take their time before beginning work on an assignment? The introductory essay says they do.

33. Procrastinate comes from the Latin *pro-* (forward) and *crastinus* (belonging to the next day). Knowing that, you can see how the word got its meaning: to put off doing something. Do you procrastinate when you've been given an assignment, or do you get straight to it?

34. A distraction is something that takes your attention from one place to another. If you're watching your favorite TV show and your little brother keeps asking you why the sky is blue, you might not welcome that particular distraction.

35. To emerge is to *come out of*. Athena emerged full-grown from her father's head, but a superior piece of writing hardly ever emerges all at once from the mind of its creator.

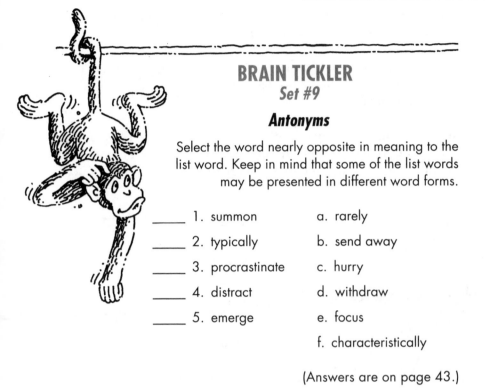

BRAIN TICKLER
Set #9

Antonyms

Select the word nearly opposite in meaning to the list word. Keep in mind that some of the list words may be presented in different word forms.

_____ 1. summon

_____ 2. typically

_____ 3. procrastinate

_____ 4. distract

_____ 5. emerge

a. rarely

b. send away

c. hurry

d. withdraw

e. focus

f. characteristically

(Answers are on page 43.)

Meet Words 36 to 40!

36. Dismayed can work either as an adjective ("When he heard the news of his sister's death, he was understandably dismayed") or as the past tense for a verb ("The news of his sister's death understandably dismayed him"). As a verb, it can mean to *sadden* or *distress*. As an adjective it means *saddened* or *distressed*.

37. Critical is an adjective with several different meanings. It suggests an attempt to judge without prejudice, to find both the faults and the strengths. A critical review of a movie will do just that. But the word sometimes has a strongly negative connotation and describes someone who tends to find fault more easily than he finds merits. A third meaning: we use "critical" to refer to something that is *decisive*. Here's an example: It was a critical moment in the ball game.

38. To be aloof is to be *distant* or emotionally uninvolved. It can be hard to warm up to such a person.

39. What is your least favorite subject in school? Do you loathe it, or is it bearable? Who teaches that class? Do you loathe him or her?

40. That which is essential is absolutely *necessary*. Food and water are essential for humans to survive. When it comes to writing, planning and revision are almost as essential.

BRAIN TICKLER
Set #10

Descriptions Inferred from Actions

Choose the vocabulary word (dismayed, critical, aloof, loathe, essential) that describes the person, animal, or thing in each example.

1. _____ When Mrs. Smith, the bank manager, took a two-week vacation from work, the whole operation of the bank just fell apart.

2. _____ Terri received a letter in the mail telling her that she had not been accepted to the college of her choice.

3. _____ Samantha does her job well, but she hasn't made any friends, probably because most people find her a little distant.

4. _____ I can't stand drivers who tailgate. There's nothing I hate as much as that.

5. _____ The decision of the Supreme Court in *Bush v. Gore* would decide the presidential election of 2000.

(Answers are on page 43.)

Meet Words 41 to 45!

41. To revise means to revisit with your eyes—to go back and see. It comes from the Latin prefix *re-* (back) and the root *visere* (to look over). That's just what you do when you revise a document or an opinion. You go back and look it over, and maybe you make some changes.

When two or pronunciations a single word are given, the order in which they

42. Ponder comes from the Latin word *ponderare*, which means "to weigh." That's exactly what you do when you ponder. You weigh something with your mind. You think it over very seriously. You *contemplate* that issue.

43. You'd probably prefer to solve a simple math problem, but a solving a complex one—one that's more *complicated*, one that has more than one side to it—would be more challenging and maybe more satisfying.

44. To determine is to reach a decision after some thought. A good writer must determine whether his piece has met all its goals, and that's not an easy task.

45. Seldom is an adverb that doesn't end in "–ly." It means *rarely* (an adverb that does end in "-ly").

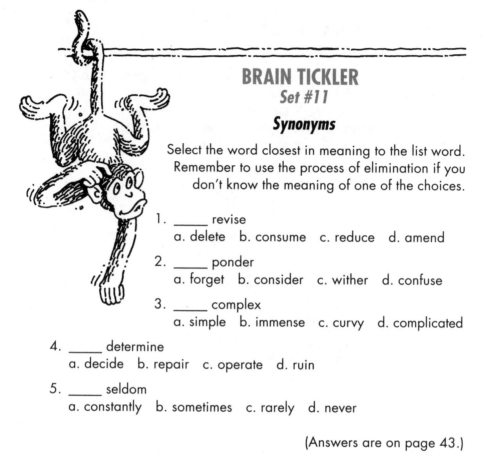

BRAIN TICKLER
Set #11

Synonyms

Select the word closest in meaning to the list word. Remember to use the process of elimination if you don't know the meaning of one of the choices.

1. _____ revise
   a. delete   b. consume   c. reduce   d. amend

2. _____ ponder
   a. forget   b. consider   c. wither   d. confuse

3. _____ complex
   a. simple   b. immense   c. curvy   d. complicated

4. _____ determine
   a. decide   b. repair   c. operate   d. ruin

5. _____ seldom
   a. constantly   b. sometimes   c. rarely   d. never

(Answers are on page 43.)

READ, READ, AND READ SOME MORE

Don't bother looking for a shortcut to a superior vocabulary. You won't find one. And the simple truth of the matter is that you already know the one time-tested strategy that's sure to work: read a lot.

When you read, you come across words whose meaning you're just not sure of. You've seen them before—maybe lots of times—but now you're seeing them again and again, and slowly, just by understanding the context in which these words are used, you are growing more certain of and more comfortable with their meaning.

You're also going to come across words whose meanings you don't know at all. When you do so, you're going to make a decision. You might decide that understanding a particular word is not essential to your understanding and enjoyment of a particular text, and therefore you won't bother to interrupt your reading to look up a word. Or you might decide the opposite. You might decide that you need to know this word right now, and you'll find its meaning in a dictionary.

The key thing for you to understand and accept is that these opportunities won't come your way unless you read frequently.

Here are simple strategies to increase your reading time and pleasure:

1. Read material you enjoy. If you're interested in sports or fashion, get your hands on *Sports Illustrated* or *In Style*. If you like the contemporary music scene, read *The Source* or *Rolling Stone*. Read young adult novels, if you enjoy those.

2. Read material that you find comfortable. It's not a matter of choosing between Shakespeare or Thomas Hardy. Don't think you need to impress anybody with the material you're reading. Even easy books will contain their fair share of words that you may find challenging.

3. Try to increase your reading time gradually. You probably know that crash diets don't work because they're impossible to keep up. The same is true of a reading routine. If you'll make small lifestyle changes—changes that don't hurt—these changes are more likely to become permanent. So, while you're eating breakfast, check out the sports section of the newspaper. Keep a couple of your favorite magazines in the TV room, so you can read an article during commercials. Try to read a few pages of that novel just before your head hits the pillow.

4. Read online. You probably do this already, right?

5. If you're traveling, pack something to read, just in case you run out of CDs to listen to.

6. Don't let reading become a chore. Read when you feel like it. Make opportunities to read, but don't let reading feel like punishment. Don't think you need to read for fifteen minutes on Monday, seventeen minutes on Tuesday, and twenty minutes on Wednesday.

7. Keep a little black book. (There is more on this in Chapter Five.)

BRAIN TICKLER
Set #12

Words in Context

Good teaching sentences provide helpful context clues. Use these clues to select the best word to complete the sentences that follow. The list words are: summon, typically, procrastinate, distraction, emerge, dismayed, critical, aloof, loathe, essential, revise, ponder, complex, determine, and seldom.

1. At first I liked the plan, but when I thought about some of its negatives, I had to _____ my opinion.

2. Some of the editorials were _____ of the mayor's proposal, but others approved of it enthusiastically.

3. You must _____ how many hours of study will earn you the grades you desire.

4. The principal _____ all the teachers to an important after-school meeting.

5. We have _____ seen such a snowy winter; it last snowed this much in 1924.

6. Some people like bananas in their pancakes, and some like chocolate chips, but everyone agrees that maple syrup is absolutely _____.

7. The exam featured mostly _____ problems. Because the study guide offered only simple ones, the students were not prepared for the actual exam.

8. When it comes to mowing the lawn, a chore Tim strongly dislikes, he has no trouble finding ways to _____.

9. Complaining that they found the candidate _____ and unemotional, the voters on Election Day did not return him to office.

10. You may _____ how a terrible event like the Holocaust could ever take place and still be no closer to really knowing the reasons.

11. Teenagers _____ spend four hours a day watching television, but it's hard to imagine that statement applying to excellent students.

12. The owners were _____ when their favorite horse failed to finish the race.

13. If we put our heads together, who knows what wonderful ideas might _____?

14. As much as I love fresh pizza straight from the oven, I _____ the very idea of yesterday's stale, reheated slices.

15. Mary was trying to concentrate on the crossword puzzle, so her daughter's crying provided an unwelcome _____.

(Answers are on page 43.)

ON YOUR OWN

If you're going to become a more serious reader, it's important for you to evaluate where you are right now. Scrutinize your own reading behavior for a week. Get some baseline information. Each night take a few minutes to complete this reading chart. It would probably be easier to think in terms of time spent on each activity. So, if on Sunday you spend forty-five minutes on reading for school, just write "45" in the designated box.

	Reading for School	Novels	Books of Nonfiction	Magazines	Newspapers	Online	Other (Specify)
Sunday							
Monday							
Tuesday							
Wednesday							
Thursday							
Friday							
Saturday							

THE LAST WORD

You know that certain words have everyday meanings, the meanings they most often have, but sometimes they have very specialized ones. You saw that in the case of summons, which can refer to a legal document. The same is true with complex. In its everyday form, "complex" is an adjective which means just about the same as "complicated" or "intricate." But, in the field of psychiatry, the word assumes another meaning: an emotional condition that influences a person's behavior. Thus an inferiority complex would refer to a poor self-image that results in a lack of confidence.

BRAIN TICKLERS—THE ANSWERS

Set #9, page 33

1. b
2. a
3. c
4. e
5. d

Set #10, page 34

1. essential
2. dismayed
3. aloof
4. loathe
5. critical

Set #11, page 36

1. d
2. b
3. d
4. a
5. c

Set #12, page 39

1. revise
2. critical
3. determine
4. summoned
5. seldom
6. essential
7. complex
8. procrastinate
9. aloof
10. ponder
11. typically
12. dismayed
13. emerge
14. loathe
15. distraction

CHAPTER FOUR

Old Folks? What Does It Mean to Be Old in the 21st Century?

Verbal Analogies

It's funny to hear children talk naively about age. "He's a nice guy," one will say, "but he's old." "Oh, how old is he?" "I don't know. Forty, I guess. Your age."

In the year 1200, forty may have been old, but it isn't any longer. For well-understood reasons, life expectancy has increased significantly in the last century. People eat healthier, smoke less, and better understand the benefits of exercise. Thanks to advances in medicine and public health, doctors do a better job treating life-threatening illnesses. They are well on their way to addressing chronic diseases like cancer and heart disease.

The result is mind-blowing. In 1900, an American could anticipate a life span of 48 years, whereas in 2000, the average life span has climbed to 75!

Naturally, this leads us to speculate, "What is the limit? How old is old?" According to records believed to be authentic, a man in Japan lived to the age of 120.

Scientists agree that the answer lies in these three factors: genetics, environment, and lifestyle. It may not be easy, but people can change their environments and their lifestyles. However, for a long time, most experts felt that little could be done about the first, genetics. Now, with recent scientific advances, there's reason to wonder whether that is true. For example, Helen Blau of Stanford University was able to modify the genetic make-up of muscle cells. These altered cells could then be injected into muscle mass, where they would produce human growth hormone. Human growth hormone, a synthetic version of the hormone produced by the pituitary gland, has been shown to reverse the effects of aging.

Skeptics say that it's silly to want to add more and more years to one's life. What matters, they assert, is the quality of that life. Enjoy yourself, they say, and let the end come when it will.

Either way, we now have reason to wonder whether Ponce de Leon's "Fountain of Youth" is more than just a myth. We seem to be closer than ever to shattering our previous conceptions of the average human life span.

Meet Words 46 to 50!

46. Naïve has an unusual pronunciation. You will notice above the "i" a pair of dots known as an umlaut. This umlaut tells you that the vowel is pronounced twice: "nie-eev." The word comes from the French *naïf*, which means natural. We say that a person's behavior or ideas are naïve when they are *childlike* and *innocent*. It's typical of a child to think naïvely that a forty-year-old is indeed old.

47. That which is significant is worthy of your attention. It's *important*. September 11, 2001, is a significant day in American history.

48. Do you go to a public school or a private one? A school is public because it belongs to the people, or to the community. Think of a major corporation, like General Electric. It's publicly owned, since many different people own shares.

49. Something that is chronic tends to last for a long time, or if it goes away, it often reappears. Doctors used to believe that the best treatment for chronic, or *recurring*, tonsillitis was to remove the sufferer's tonsils.

50. Thanks to advances in diet and health care, you can anticipate, or *look forward to*, a longer life span. When you turn the calendar to June, you probably anticipate eagerly the arrival of summer.

BRAIN TICKLER
Set #13

Nuts or Not?

Read each sentence to decide if the underlined vocabulary word is used correctly in context. If the meaning is ludicrous (or ridiculous), write "Nuts" in the blank space. If the sentence makes sense, write "Not" in the blank space.

1. _____ Sandra had a <u>naïve</u> view of the world: she was suspicious of everyone and even questioned obvious acts of kindness.

2. _____ In trying to determine which patients to treat first, the doctors had to figure out which injuries were <u>significant</u> and which were slight.

3. _____ Whether Matt earns an A on the science exam is a matter of great <u>public</u> interest, as he discusses his test scores only with his best friend Earl.

4. _____ Terri's rash had all the makings of a <u>chronic</u> condition: it appeared that one time . . . and never again.

5. _____ The three-game series was completely sold out, and the announcers correctly concluded that the fans eagerly <u>anticipated</u> these important games.

(Answers are on page 58.)

Meet Words 51 to 55!

51. It's only natural that we speculate or *wonder* if there's any built-in limit to how long humans can live. Speculate has a specialized meaning, too. In the business world, investors speculate; they take chances. They purchase properties or stocks, hoping to make a large profit when they sell them. The flip side to that is that investors who speculate risk seeing their investments turn into losses.

52. Something that is authentic is the real deal. It's *genuine* and, for that reason, trustworthy. An authentic Abraham Lincoln autograph would probably be very valuable.

53. To modify is to *change* in form or content. If you modify your diet, you are changing the amounts and kinds of foods you eat. If you modify your lifestyle, maybe you are trying to squeeze in some exercise. (In grammar, we say that a modifier, such as an adjective, changes or limits the meaning of the word it modifies.)

54. Alter is a verb that means just about the same as "modify." Therefore, altered (used as an adjective in the introductory essay: "altered genes") means *changed*. If there is a difference between "modify" and "alter," it's a matter of degree. Usually, "modify" refers to a slight change, whereas "alter" may or may not. If you need to have some alterations (noun form) in a recently purchased suit, you will probably bring the garment to a tailor.

55. A mass is a quantity of matter that comes together to form a particular substance, as in muscle mass. It can also mean a large quantity: a mass of protesters assembled in the town square. Mass also has a specialized meaning, referring to a religious service. The verb form of the word, "amass," means to gather.

BRAIN TICKLER
Set #14

Words in Context

Use the correct forms of list words 51 to 55 (speculate, authentic, modify, altered, mass) to complete this paragraph.

No one can deny how beautiful diamonds can be, but an untrained observer might not be able to tell whether a stone is even (1) _____. Have you ever seen a brilliantly shining diamond on a woman's finger? It's hard to realize that once it was simply a (2) _____ of coal. Tons and tons of pressure have so dramatically (3) _____ its appearance. A non-expert can only (4) _____ about the steps a gem cutter must take in order to (5) _____ the stone to its final shape.

(Answers are on page 58.)

Meet Words 56 to 60!

56. That which is synthetic is not found in nature. It is *artificial*. The synthetic human growth hormone that scientists inject into muscle mass has been created in a laboratory.

57. A person who is skeptical doubts and questions. A skeptic is likely to wonder whether a statement generally accepted by others is actually true.

58. Assert has two meanings. Skeptics assert—or *claim*—that what matters is not the number of years, but the quality of the life. A second frequently used meaning is to insist upon one's rights. When the coach benched him, James asserted himself and asked for a chance to reclaim his starting position. You will also see the adjective form—"assertive"—used to describe a person who is willing to step forward in this way.

59. A myth can also be one of two things. Its most common meaning is that of a *story*, a *legend*, such as the ancient Greek myth of Hercules. However, because such a story often stretches the boundary of truth, myth can also refer to a made-up story, or a *falsehood*.

60. Conception has three common meanings. Its first, one that appears in the introductory essay ("previous conceptions of the human life span") refers to an *idea*. A second, closely related meaning refers to academic *understanding*. Despite the teacher's clear explanation, the student had no conception of the material. A third meaning refers to a *beginning*. The project was conceived in 1998, but it took the agency seven years to complete it.

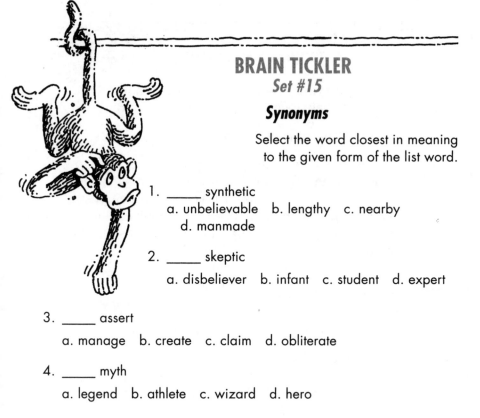

BRAIN TICKLER
Set #15

Synonyms

Select the word closest in meaning
to the given form of the list word.

1. _____ synthetic
   a. unbelievable   b. lengthy   c. nearby
   d. manmade

2. _____ skeptic
   a. disbeliever   b. infant   c. student   d. expert

3. _____ assert
   a. manage   b. create   c. claim   d. obliterate

4. _____ myth
   a. legend   b. athlete   c. wizard   d. hero

5. _____ conception
   a. attempt   b. victory   c. idea   d. simplicity

(Answers are on page 58.)

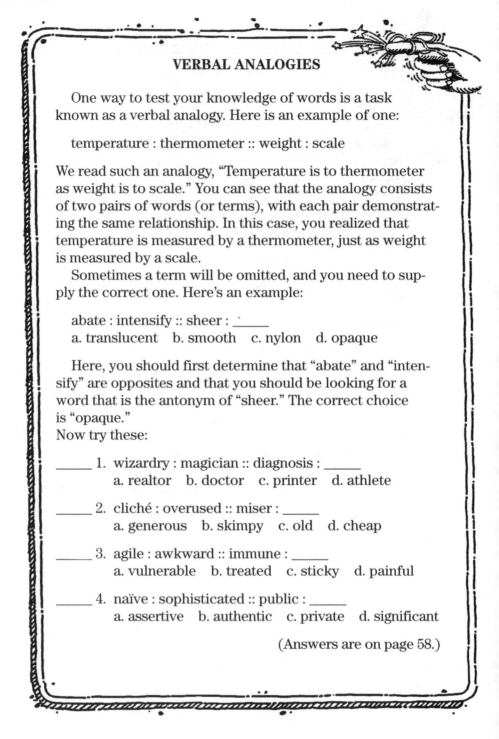

VERBAL ANALOGIES

One way to test your knowledge of words is a task known as a verbal analogy. Here is an example of one:

temperature : thermometer :: weight : scale

We read such an analogy, "Temperature is to thermometer as weight is to scale." You can see that the analogy consists of two pairs of words (or terms), with each pair demonstrating the same relationship. In this case, you realized that temperature is measured by a thermometer, just as weight is measured by a scale.

Sometimes a term will be omitted, and you need to supply the correct one. Here's an example:

abate : intensify :: sheer : _____
a. translucent   b. smooth   c. nylon   d. opaque

Here, you should first determine that "abate" and "intensify" are opposites and that you should be looking for a word that is the antonym of "sheer." The correct choice is "opaque."

Now try these:

_____ 1. wizardry : magician :: diagnosis : _____
   a. realtor   b. doctor   c. printer   d. athlete

_____ 2. cliché : overused :: miser : _____
   a. generous   b. skimpy   c. old   d. cheap

_____ 3. agile : awkward :: immune : _____
   a. vulnerable   b. treated   c. sticky   d. painful

_____ 4. naïve : sophisticated :: public : _____
   a. assertive   b. authentic   c. private   d. significant

(Answers are on page 58.)

BRAIN TICKLER
Set #16

Words in Context

As you search for the appropriate list word, remember to search for context clues. The list words are: naïve, significant, public, chronic, anticipate, speculate, authentic, modify, altered, mass, synthetic, skeptic, assert, myth, and conception.

1. When Jim's knee pain became _____, he finally agreed to the operation that would relieve it once and for all.

2. Watching the troubling events on the evening news will cause _____ youngsters to examine their innocent ideas about the world.

3. Even though legislation had given African Americans the right to vote, in certain sections of the country they still needed to _____ that right.

4. Thomas Jefferson believed that _____ education was the key to democracy; if schools educated all the nation's citizens, then those citizens would be able to exercise their rights wisely.

5. The tailor _____ my brother's jacket so that it fit me properly.

6. Scientists _____ about the effects of global warming and wonder how higher daily temperatures will affect life on Earth.

7. You may have a certain _____ about what high school will be like, but it's better for you to keep an open mind about new experiences.

8. An expert said the Babe Ruth autograph was _____ and therefore worth a great deal of money.

9. Doctors may dismiss a few cases of the illness, but they become concerned when a(n) _____ number of patients become ill.

10. The mayor said that a stepped-up police presence would reduce crime, but _____ were convinced that the recommended police presence was not nearly large enough.

11. Some people claim that Babe Ruth's "called shot" home run in the 1932 World Series was just a(n) _____, but some who attended the game said it actually happened.

12. The surgeon found a large _____ on Jeanine's kidney and had to remove it.

13. A few students in the class could not work as quickly as the others, so the teacher had to _____ the test, creating a slightly shorter version for this group.

14. As spring wends its way through May and June, students eagerly _____ the arrival of summer vacation.

15. The shirt's label indicated that it was made from _____ fibers, not from cotton or wool, which are found in nature.

(Answers are on page 58.)

ON YOUR OWN

At first glance, the thought of living a long life is a very attractive one. If we look at the amazing difference in life spans from 1900 to 2000, it's hard to find any negatives at all.

But what would happen if life could be extended even more? By a lot? Certainly, a significant number of problems would result. For example, it stands to reason that the population of the world would grow much faster than it ever has before, which might lead to other problems.

Conduct a little research on your own. Go online or consult an encyclopedia, and see if you can find some of these problems. Using at least five of this chapter's list words, write a good body paragraph in which you describe some possible negative outcomes of longer life spans.

THE LAST WORD

The word synthesis (it's a noun) refers to the putting together of parts to make a whole. When these parts are actually chemicals, the end product is synthetic. "Synthesis" also has a specialized meaning. It refers to a thought process, in which one takes several facts and assembles them into an idea. A researcher will consult various sources, obtain information from each, and synthesize (a verb) all that material in the paper he or she writes. (Of course, as long as the researcher has not plagiarized, we do not refer to the work as "synthetic.")

BRAIN TICKLERS—THE ANSWERS

Set #13, page 49

1. nuts
2. not
3. nuts
4. nuts
5. not

Set #14, page 51

1. authentic
2. mass
3. altered
4. speculate
5. modify

Set #15, page 53

1. d
2. a
3. c
4. a
5. c

Verbal Analogies, page 54

1. b
2. d
3. a
4. c

Set #16, page 55

1. chronic
2. naïve
3. assert
4. public
5. altered
6. speculate
7. conception
8. authentic
9. significant
10. skeptics
11. myth
12. mass
13. modify
14. anticipate
15. synthetic

CHAPTER FIVE

The Tale of the Teaching Tyrant
Starting Your Own Black Book

To look at her, you'd never suspect the truth. Physically she was not imposing at all. She was middle-aged and diminutive, barely five feet tall. Neither her appearance nor her plain attire would draw anyone's attention. She spoke in a voice slightly high-pitched, which she never, ever raised beyond a comfortable speaking level. (It was tough sometimes for students sitting in the back of the room to make out what she said, but they were unwilling to provoke her by raising their hands and suggesting that she speak more loudly.)

She was the Teaching Tyrant, the acknowledged queen of her classroom.

There were teachers in her school literally twice her size—three-hundred-pound brutes in impressively tailored suits, who could not exert anywhere near this kind of control over their classrooms. How did she do it? The answer is simple: intimidation.

The first day of school she inflicted upon her students a set of rules, which had to be followed precisely. One such rule: students could not cross out their written work. To prove her point, within a day or two, she assigned homework. The following day, she ordered the papers passed forward and collected them from the first student sitting in each row.

She glanced through the papers from the first row. She selected one from the bunch. With just her thumb and forefinger, she held it at a distance from her body, as if it were a vile piece of garbage. "This," she remarked, "is not acceptable," and she returned it to the student.

The girl, evidently eager to please her new teacher, had worked very hard on the assignment. She filled both sides of the page with dark ink. Perhaps in her zeal, she had forgotten the cross-out rule and neatly blackened a few words on the sheet. The girl was humiliated, and she began to cry.

In this way, students learned to fear their new teacher. In this way, they succumbed to her rules. The class was quiet. Students who would readily misbehave in other classes remained mute in this one. The Teaching Tyrant had won the battle—and many battles, too, that would never be fought.

But she lost the war.

Learning doesn't happen when students are so afraid of the teacher that they sit on their hands. Learning results from the free exchange of ideas. Students know that ideas cannot be exchanged freely when they are forced to conform to senseless rules.

Meet Words 61 to 65!

61. To impose means to place a burden (such as a tax) or to force oneself upon another. Therefore, imposing means making an impression because of one's size or strength. Certainly, a teacher can be physically imposing, but the Teaching Tyrant was not.

62. Diminutive is the adjective form of the verb "diminish," which means to make smaller. Something or someone who is diminutive is very *small*.

63. Your attire is, quite simply, your *clothing*. You can also use the word as a verb: Laura believed it was important to attire her children neatly.

64. To provoke is to *stir up* some feeling in another person. Students in the Teaching Tyrant's class were unwilling to ask unnecessary questions, since this might provoke her to anger. You might also be familiar with the adjective form of the word, provocative, which means tending to excite. A person's language can be provocative. Some schools institute dress codes because school officials feel students dress too provocatively.

65. If you haven't figured it out by now, a tyrant is a cruel, absolute ruler. You are certainly familiar with the dinosaur tyrannosaurus, a tyrant in his own time.

BRAIN TICKLER
Set #17

Verbal Analogies

As you answer these, remember to determine the relationship between the given pair. Then create that same relationship with the second pair.

1. _____ millionaire : poor :: tyrant :
   a. government   b. war-like   c. kindly   d. taxes

2. _____ diminutive : huge :: grain of sand :
   a. water   b. skyscraper   c. battery   d. immense

3. _____ shell : nut :: attire :
   a. shoes   b. umbrella   c. body   d. covering

4. _____ imposing : unimpressive :: provoke :
   a. stir up   b. bore   c. remove   d. investigate

(Answers are on page 71.)

Meet Words 66 to 70!

66. To acknowledge is to *admit* or *recognize*. (You can see the root word "know" right in the middle.) The Teaching Tyrant was the acknowledged—or accepted—queen of her classroom because everyone knew it.

67. Literal comes from the Latin word *litera*, or "letter," and means actual or factual. When we say that there were teachers literally twice her size, we actually mean twice her size. Sometimes we say that a person is being too literal when he fails to recognize that language is being used figuratively. Consider this example. One person says, "Did you see that

tennis match? He crushed him like a gnat!" The second replies, "Did he swat him or step on him?" That second person is certainly being a bit too literal.

Major Mistake Territory!

Speakers and writers sometimes use the words "literal" or "literally" when they mean something else. Here's an example: "She was such a genius that her brain was literally larger than anyone else's body!" That's rather unlikely, unless her skull was large enough to contain such a mass. Sometimes you see these words misused when people employ figurative language—similes and metaphors. Here's an example: "He literally devoured the Harry Potter series." That, too, is unlikely . . . unless he's a goat!

68. To exert means to *use* or *apply.* If you're giving someone a massage, you will exert pressure upon that person's shoulders. The Teaching Tyrant somehow managed to exert complete control without ever raising her voice.

69. To intimidate means to *frighten.* When Dwight Howard walks onto the court, the opposing center must be intimidated. The Teaching Tyrant, on the other hand, managed the same thing without Howard's immense size.

70. Inflict comes from the Latin word *infigere* (*in-* means on or against, and *-figere* means to strike). It means to give or cause by striking. A boxer tries to inflict pain upon his opponent. The Teaching Tyrant inflicted upon her students a set of rules, which soon resulted in much pain.

BRAIN TICKLER
Set #18

Descriptions Inferred from Comments

Choose the vocabulary word from these list words (intimidated, acknowledge, literal, inflict, exert) that describes the person making the comment.

1. _____ "I need to train harder—I need to push myself—if I'm going to run a six-minute mile."

2. _____ "I've never tried skiing, and I'm a little afraid. I could fall and hurt my knee, or I could crash into a tree."

3. _____ "When you said you lived in a drafty old barn, I expected to find bales of hay and cows and chickens."

4. _____ "Even though I don't like her personally, I have to admit that she's done a good job."

5. _____ "As a linebacker, it's my job to punish the other team's ball carriers, and that's what I like to do."

(Answers are on page 71.)

Meet Words 71 to 75!

71. That which is vile is so *unpleasant* as to seem practically evil. When the Teaching Tyrant held a paper with cross-outs, she treated it as if it were a piece of garbage. Holding garbage in your hands? Now that's vile.

72. To humiliate someone is to put that person down, to *disgrace* him. It's stronger than just embarrassing someone, and it hurts more.

73. To succumb means to *give in* or *surrender*. Students had little choice but to succumb to the tyranny of the Teaching Tyrant—or else deal with the humiliation that was sure to follow.

74. When a person is mute, he is *silent*, perhaps because he is incapable of making a sound. Sometimes the word is used as a noun, to describe just such a person. It can also be a verb, meaning "to silence."

75. When a person decides to conform, that person will follow the rules and customs of a given place. A conformist is a person who wears the popular jeans and listens to the popular music. A nonconformist follows his own rules.

BRAIN TICKLER
Set #19

Extremes

Think about words that suggest extremes. Would you rather see an *interesting* movie or a *fascinating* one? Each of the following sentences contains a list word and one paired with it. Circle the word that suggests an extreme.

1. The Teaching Tyrant's remarks were so unpleasant/vile that the students soon learned to avoid her nasty responses.

2. He was a bad-tempered politician who took pleasure in humiliating/criticizing his opponents.

3. Trailing by ten runs, the team stopped trying and soon permitted/succumbed to defeat.

4. The old saying, "Children should be seen and not heard," suggests that a good child should remain soft-spoken/mute.

5. If you wish to conform to/consider the school's dress code, you must wear a shirt and tie every day.

(Answers are on page 71.)

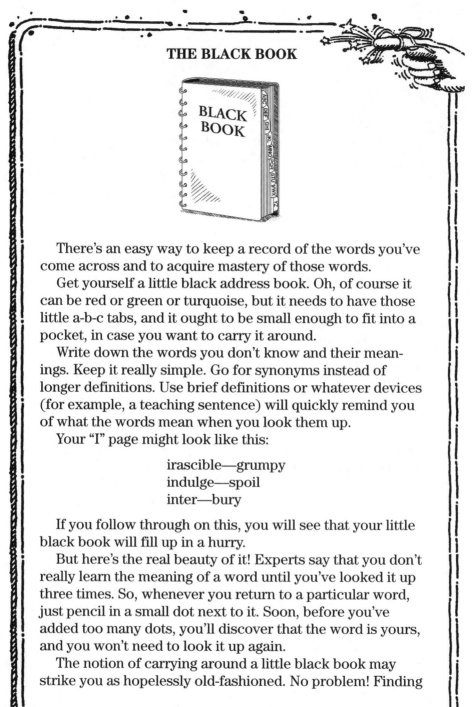

THE BLACK BOOK

There's an easy way to keep a record of the words you've come across and to acquire mastery of those words.

Get yourself a little black address book. Oh, of course it can be red or green or turquoise, but it needs to have those little a-b-c tabs, and it ought to be small enough to fit into a pocket, in case you want to carry it around.

Write down the words you don't know and their meanings. Keep it really simple. Go for synonyms instead of longer definitions. Use brief definitions or whatever devices (for example, a teaching sentence) will quickly remind you of what the words mean when you look them up.

Your "I" page might look like this:

> irascible—grumpy
> indulge—spoil
> inter—bury

If you follow through on this, you will see that your little black book will fill up in a hurry.

But here's the real beauty of it! Experts say that you don't really learn the meaning of a word until you've looked it up three times. So, whenever you return to a particular word, just pencil in a small dot next to it. Soon, before you've added too many dots, you'll discover that the word is yours, and you won't need to look it up again.

The notion of carrying around a little black book may strike you as hopelessly old-fashioned. No problem! Finding a hi-tech substitute will not be difficult. As long as your hand-held device contains a writing or spreadsheet program, you can easily keep an electronic black book. The most important thing is that it's with you wherever you go.

In any case, don't be surprised if your little black book becomes the kind of object that you'll carry with you for a very long time.

BRAIN TICKLER
Set #20

Words in Context

Choose the correct list word to complete the sentence. Look for context clues! The list words are: imposing, diminutive, attire, provoke, tyrant, acknowledged, literally, exert, intimidate, inflict, vile, humiliated, succumbed, mute, and conform.

1. The boxers stood in the center of the ring, staring into each other's eyes, each punishing brute attempting to _____ the other.

2. Hoping to _____ a response from her mother, Jessie raked her fork through her dinner plate but rarely brought a portion to her mouth.

3. Mrs. Stephens asked a hard question about World War I, and the class sat there _____, unable to offer a knowledgeable response.

4. Theresa was a wise supervisor, who knew when and how much pressure to _____ upon her employees.

5. The taste of the sour milk was so _____ that he spit it out as soon as it touched his lips.

6. Carole, realizing it would be a good idea to _____ to the dress code of her office, purchased five new business suits before she started the job.

7. The Statue of Liberty is a(n) _____ sight, as it towers above every ship that enters New York Harbor.

8. Tyrone Bogues, at 5'3", would have been short in most circumstances, but on an NBA court, playing along with nine giants, he appeared extremely _____.

9. The _____ you wear to a wedding is obviously a lot dressier than what you would wear to school.

10. The smells coming from the kitchen were so appetizing that the children were _____ drooling in anticipation of the meal.

11. Jeremy was the _____ leader of the group, since the other members recognized his superior intelligence and strength of character.

12. Pitching a complete baseball game _____ a lot of pain on the shoulder, which is why pitchers routinely ice their shoulders after they leave the game.

13. In most matters, Dad ruled the family democratically, but when it came to curfews, he was an absolute _____.

14. Because of her diet, Abby tried to avoid unnecessary carbs, but she _____ immediately to the tempting seven-layer cake.

15. Mr. Brandt certainly _____ Tim when he discussed his failing grade in front of the whole class.

(Answers are on page 71.)

ON YOUR OWN

You've had a lot of experience with teachers, enough to know the good from the bad. If a new teacher came to you looking for advice on how to make a favorable impression, what kind of advice would you give? Write a paragraph, and be sure to use at least five words from this chapter's new words.

THE LAST WORD

You can find in this chapter's list words several "words within words," and having done so you can learn more than one word at a time. You already noticed that "know" and "knowledge" lie within acknowledge, but you certainly knew those words first. That might not be the case with intimidate. Couched within that word is its root, "timid," which means "shy" or "fearful." You could say that in the Teaching Tyrant's class, bold students became timid ones. Here's another one: diminutive. Can you figure out which word lies within? (Hint: it isn't "dim"!)

BRAIN TICKLERS—THE ANSWERS

Set #17, page 63

1. c
2. b
3. c
4. b

Set #18, page 65

1. exert
2. intimidated
3. literal
4. acknowledge
5. inflict

Set #19, page 67

1. vile
2. humiliating
3. succumbed
4. mute
5. conform to

Set #20, page 69

1. intimidate
2. provoke
3. mute
4. exert
5. vile
6. conform
7. imposing
8. diminutive
9. attire
10. literally
11. acknowledged
12. inflicts
13. tyrant
14. succumbed
15. humiliated

CHAPTER SIX

The Newest Thing

Using a Dictionary

Potatoes

Are we a nation obsessed with novelty?

Not everyone loves the newest thing, but most of us do . . . eventually.

Think back to the first time you encountered someone using a cell phone. Did you have any idea what to make of it? What was that strange object jammed against a person's ear? Why was that person speaking loudly on the street or in the supermarket? Why was he chatting publicly about matters that should have been discussed discreetly?

Did you approve of this behavior? Did you say to yourself, "I just have to acquire one of these as soon as I can"? Or did you denounce this strange apparatus and its user? Did you think him uncouth? After all, what right did he have to intrude upon everyone else's public space, this showoff with his fancy new possession?

And then came another major problem. How could adults possibly drive and use phones simultaneously?

The passage of time permits two events. Those eager to convert to a culture of cell phones can take that step, and because many do, what once was shockingly new eventually seems common. This event leads to another. Those once shocked and offended by cell phone use and users grow to tolerate what had once been insufferable.

This brings us to the final stage, when even the most outspoken critics concede that cell phones are not that bad—and become cell phone users themselves. Maybe the cell phone companies make an offer they just can't refuse. Maybe they find themselves in situations where having a cell phone would have helped. Maybe they just say to themselves, "Oh, why not?"

Before long, every street and every store is filled with cell phone users, ranging in age from eight to eighty.

Before long, everyone wonders, "How did I ever live without one?"

And then the last stage: the newest, newest thing, the thing that replaces the cell phone and makes it obsolete.

And the cycle begins again.

Meet Words 76 to 80!

76. Obsessed is the past participle form of the verb, "to obsess." When you are obsessed with something, you just can't get it out of your mind. Are you one of these people who are obsessed with the newest thing?

77. Novelty is the noun form of the adjective "novel," which you are more likely to see and hear. Novelty means *newness* or *freshness* or *originality*. Sometimes it refers to some object or activity that is new or fresh or original.

78. To encounter is to *meet* or *experience*. Do you remember the first time you encountered (or experienced) a cell phone? You might encounter (or meet) some of your friends leaving the movie theater. Sometimes the word is used as a noun. Meeting the inventor made for a fascinating encounter.

79. Discreetly is the adverb form of the adjective discreet. When you do something discreetly, you are very careful about what you say or do. Having private conversations in public places is not behaving discreetly.

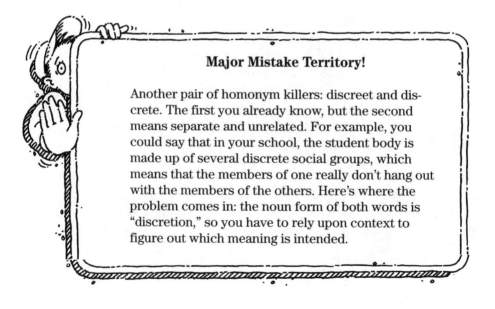

Major Mistake Territory!

Another pair of homonym killers: discreet and discrete. The first you already know, but the second means separate and unrelated. For example, you could say that in your school, the student body is made up of several discrete social groups, which means that the members of one really don't hang out with the members of the others. Here's where the problem comes in: the noun form of both words is "discretion," so you have to rely upon context to figure out which meaning is intended.

80. To acquire something is simply to *get* or *obtain* one. Can you think of something you just absolutely had to acquire? The noun form of the word is acquisition. A person who needs to own lots of items is acquisitive.

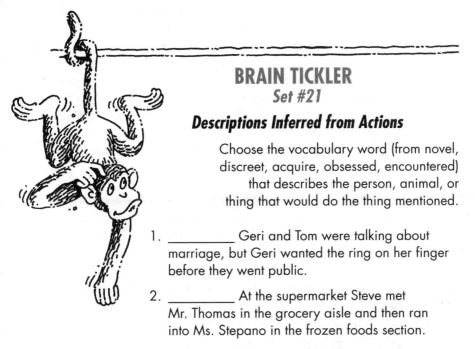

BRAIN TICKLER
Set #21

Descriptions Inferred from Actions

Choose the vocabulary word (from novel, discreet, acquire, obsessed, encountered) that describes the person, animal, or thing that would do the thing mentioned.

1. _____ Geri and Tom were talking about marriage, but Geri wanted the ring on her finger before they went public.

2. _____ At the supermarket Steve met Mr. Thomas in the grocery aisle and then ran into Ms. Stepano in the frozen foods section.

3. _____ Jeremy whispered his test grade in Serena's ear so no one else could hear.

4. _____ After Paul enjoyed *The Outsiders,* he read every single word that S. E. Hinton ever wrote.

5. _____ Rick picked up his new car, and he couldn't get over some of the vehicle's features, such as the rain-sensitive wipers, which he'd never seen before.

(Answers are on page 86.)

Meet Words 81 to 85!

81. To denounce is to *criticize* very strongly. A person who failed to appreciate cell phones might have denounced them. In another, related sense denounce can mean to accuse someone publicly. The governor's critics denounced him as a thief. The noun form of the word is "denunciation."

82. An apparatus is an *instrument, material,* or *tool* used for a specific purpose. A cell phone is an apparatus used for what is now a well-known purpose. Some apparatuses are technical, like a surgeon's scalpel, whereas a simple screwdriver can be just the apparatus you need to repair something around the house.

83. A person who is uncouth is *ill-mannered* or *impolite.* A person could demonstrate uncouth behavior because he doesn't know any better or because he doesn't care to behave politely.

84. To intrude is to force oneself upon another without invitation or permission. You might be angry with your parents if they enter your room without knocking and thereby intrude upon your privacy. In the introductory passage, the opposite occurs. A person conducting a private conversation intrudes upon people's public space. You will see the noun forms rather often. One who intrudes is an intruder. The act itself is an intrusion.

85. When two things occur at the same time, we say they happened simultaneously. Simultaneously driving and talking on a cell phone can be a recipe for disaster. If the phone and the doorbell ring simultaneously, which would you answer first?

BRAIN TICKLER
Set #22

Words in Context

Use the correct forms of list words 81 to 85
(denounce, apparatus, uncouth, intruder,
simultaneously) to complete this paragraph.

Do you think that the inventions of the fork and spoon occurred
(1) _____, or do you think one came before the other? If you
think the latter may be true, which (2) _____ do you think arrived
first? Imagine a time in our history when eating with one's hands was
considered polite. At such a time, the first fork- or spoon-user had to
be considered (3) _____. It probably took a lot of nerve to bring
one's own fork or spoon to the home of a less cultured host. Would the
host (4) _____ such bold, unmannerly behavior? Would an early
fork- or spoon-user be treated like a(n) (5) _____ and not invited
back any time soon?

(Answers are on page 86.)

Meet Words 86 to 90!

86. Convert is an interesting verb with a couple of closely related meanings. To convert can mean to *change* or *transfer*. For example, any writing program will easily convert one font to another. It also has a narrower range of meaning. Convert can mean to change the way a person thinks or acts. For example, John converted to a new religion. A person who undergoes such a change is called a convert. The act is a conversion.

87. At first, cell phone users may have offended some, but eventually those people learned to tolerate, or deal with, them. To tolerate something is to *allow* it to be. In another sense, to tolerate means to respect without necessarily agreeing. For example, you can tolerate the beliefs of another religion without necessarily being a believer yourself.

88. If you discover something that you just can't tolerate, you would describe it as insufferable. All sorts of situations could be considered insufferable: summer heat and humidity, a boring class that never seems to end, an unpleasant lecture from a teacher or parent, or the taste of something vile (eel? sour milk? overcooked veggies?).

89. To concede is to *give in* or to *admit* something that you had not wanted to admit. If your team is losing a game by a ridiculous margin, you might just concede defeat instead of playing until the bitter end. Even the harshest critics of cell phone users eventually come around and concede that cell phones are very useful . . . and sometimes lots of fun.

90. Something that is obsolete is very, very far from being up-to-date. It's beyond *old-fashioned*. The arrival of the automobile made the horse and buggy obsolete. And have you ever seen a rotary phone, one of those ancient models with the circular dialer? Talk about obsolete.

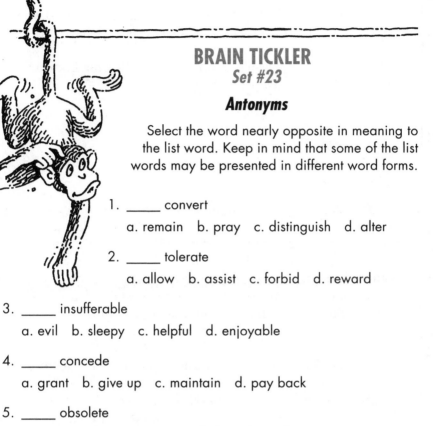

BRAIN TICKLER
Set #23

Antonyms

Select the word nearly opposite in meaning to the list word. Keep in mind that some of the list words may be presented in different word forms.

1. _____ convert
   a. remain   b. pray   c. distinguish   d. alter

2. _____ tolerate
   a. allow   b. assist   c. forbid   d. reward

3. _____ insufferable
   a. evil   b. sleepy   c. helpful   d. enjoyable

4. _____ concede
   a. grant   b. give up   c. maintain   d. pay back

5. _____ obsolete
   a. ancient   b. current   c. symbolic   d. worthy

(Answers are on page 86.)

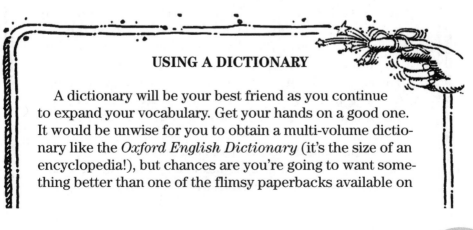

USING A DICTIONARY

A dictionary will be your best friend as you continue to expand your vocabulary. Get your hands on a good one. It would be unwise for you to obtain a multi-volume dictionary like the *Oxford English Dictionary* (it's the size of an encyclopedia!), but chances are you're going to want something better than one of the flimsy paperbacks available on the mass market. A good hardcover dictionary may cost you $20 or more, but it is money well spent. You will have it for years.

A quality dictionary will offer you the following information about the word you look up:

- pronunciation key
- part of speech
- etymology (word origin)
- definitions
- synonyms

Let's take a look at a sample entry for the word "banish."

---

banish (ban' ish) *v.t.* [M.E. *banischen*] 1. to put out of the country as a punishment   2. to send away   3. to put out of one's mind SYN.—**exile** implies being forced to leave one's own country; to **deport** is to send out of a country

---

Let's take a closer look at pronunciation. First, the word is broken into syllables. Second, you will see that the first syllable is accented (') and therefore receives the stress. That means it receives a little more emphasis than the second. Third, you know that in English a single letter can represent several sounds. The "a" in "fat" is different from the "a" in "sofa." You will find on the bottom of the dictionary page a pronunciation key. This key will show you how letters and symbols are used in other words. "Banish" is quite straightforward, but, if you weren't sure about how to pronounce the "a," you could look on the bottom of the page and find the word "fat," which would tell you that the "a" is pronounced the same in both words.

The etymologies may not be of major interest to you, but you may be interested to discover that words share certain roots, or that a word like "mentor" actually comes from a Greek legend.

The definitions are generally listed in order of their usage—the most common definition is given first, the least common (and most specialized) last. When you look up words, try to find the given definition that best satisfies the word's meaning in that particular context.

As this book has already indicated, words have shades of meaning, and a good dictionary will show you that synonyms are not exact fits. In the case above, neither "exile" nor "deport" is a perfect match for "banish," but both come pretty close.

Later in this book, we'll take a look at some of the online (or electronic) dictionaries available to you.

BRAIN TICKLER
Set #24

Words in Context

Choose the correct list word to complete the sentence. Look for context clues! List words are: obsessed, novelty, encounter, discreetly, acquire, denounce, apparatus, uncouth, intrude, simultaneously, convert, tolerate, insufferable, concede, and obsolete.

1. The invention of central air conditioning did not make individual air conditioning units _____ because changing from individual units to central air was very expensive.

2. Saying he had no respect for someone who would steal another's words and thoughts, Mr. Danson chose to _____ plagiarism on the very first day of classes.

3. On his trip to Europe, Felix became so _____ with espresso coffee that he bought himself an espresso maker as soon as he returned to the States.

4. Paula never learned to _____ the warm, sticky Miami summers and eventually purchased a summer home in Maine.

5. For Alex and Andrea, the food at this particular restaurant was so delicious and exciting that every visit offered some of the surprise and _____ of their very first time there.

6. The missionaries wanted to _____ the natives to Christianity, but some were not eager to give up their own beliefs.

7. I wanted to take Jessica to that fancy French restaurant, but I was afraid that her _____ manners would embarrass both of us.

8. As soon as Phil lost his queen, he saw that his opponent's advantage was too great and decided to _____ the match.

9. If you travel to a different country, you are likely to _____ customs that you will not find at home.

10. It was Matthew's goal to _____ his own luxury automobile— to see it resting in his driveway—and before long his dream came true.

11. I suggest that you discuss this matter _____, since you don't want others hearing this sensitive material.

12. Two students raised their hands _____, so the teacher called on the student who spoke less frequently.

13. Because of drought, political tyranny, and famine, living conditions in the region were completely _____.

14. This particular _____ is very attractive to look at, but because it consists of many parts is difficult to repair.

15. Please knock on the door so that you do not _____ upon my privacy.

(Answers are on page 86.)

ON YOUR OWN

Write a good body paragraph about something that once was new but is no longer. You can write about a fad (a custom or style that people are interested in for a short time). If you do, you write about an activity or a clothing style or a type of music. You can also write about some invention that was the rage for a short period of time. Be sure to use at least five list words from this chapter.

THE LAST WORD

For some reason it can be hard to understand accented and unaccented syllables. This is a handy skill, though, as you attempt to pronounce new words correctly. (It also comes in handy when you study meter in poetry.) Let's take a look at the list word simultaneously. That's a pretty long word. It consists of six syllables. Say it a few times slowly. Try to figure out which syllables get the stress. One way to do this is to exaggerate the stressed syllables. If it sounds only a little bit weird, then you're probably doing it correctly. However, if it sounds like another word entirely, then you're not on the right track.

The correct answer is si' mul ta' ne ous ly. Only the first and third syllables get the stress.

Try a few of the other list words. Use your dictionary to check your answers.

BRAIN TICKLERS—THE ANSWERS

Set #21, page 77

1. acquire
2. encountered
3. discreet
4. obsessed
5. novel

Set #22, page 79

1. simultaneously
2. apparatus
3. uncouth
4. denounce
5. intruder

Set #23, page 81

1. a
2. c
3. d
4. c
5. b

Set #24, page 83

1. obsolete
2. denounce
3. obsessed
4. tolerate
5. novelty
6. convert
7. uncouth
8. concede
9. encounter
10. acquire
11. discreetly
12. simultaneously
13. insufferable
14. apparatus
15. intrude

CHAPTER SEVEN

Where Have All the Words Gone?

A Brief History of Our Language

Would you like to conduct an interesting experiment? Go to a used bookstore, and get your hands on an old magazine, something pre-1950s, if you can. Then take a quick look at some of the ads. You will not have to peruse them, because that one glance will alert you to a very obvious characteristic. You might find a small illustration or a pleasant black-and-white photograph, but for the most part these ads are dense with text. The page is filled with words. It would take you five or ten minutes to read the entire ad.

Now pick up a contemporary magazine and find an ad, any ad. You will notice the difference immediately. Gone are all the words. Gone! They have vanished, it seems, replaced by images.

Let's compare them more closely.

The older one happens to be an automobile ad. Its ten paragraphs provide in great detail the reasons you should buy the car. You will learn how the car accelerates and how well it maneuvers in traffic. You will learn how its stability contributes to smooth turning. You will read about the manufacturer's promise: you'll never feel a drop of remorse for deciding to own this car.

The modern ad is also black-and-white (although most are color), but that is where the similarity ends. The name of the car company appears at the top right corner of the page. At the adjacent corner is a single paragraph. It is hard to call it a paragraph, though, because paragraphs consist of sentences, yet this paragraph comprises only pieces of sentences. It advertises a handful of features (for example, a navigation system) that had not been invented when the earlier ad appeared. There is not an abundance of information. In fact, if you want more, there is a dot.com address you can investigate on your own. That's it for the text.

The image does the rest of the talking: a black vehicle on a black background. Its chrome and glass are perfectly lighted to create a sense of power and mystery. Its manufacturer obviously believes that power and mystery are more important than information.

Think for a second about that first ad. If you came across that ad today, would you take the time to read it? Would you find ten minutes in your busy day—a day filled with school and friends and homework and chores and e-mail and IMs— to acquire all that information about the car? Probably not. But when that ad first appeared, the magazine's readers surely found the time to read it. Can you imagine a world paced so leisurely that readers would donate valuable time to an advertisement? It is indeed hard to imagine.

Meet Words 91 to 95!

91. To peruse something is to read or *examine* it very carefully. An old-time ad begs you to peruse it, but for a modern ad a quick look will do.

92. That *quick look* is called a glance. The word is often used as a verb. To glance means not only to look quickly, but it can also mean to strike something at an angle and then bounce off. Even if your car just glances off another, you won't be happy about the body damage.

93. When we say something is dense, we mean that its parts are packed tightly together. It is *thick* and *hard to penetrate*. Perhaps, for this same reason, when we say that someone is dense, we mean that he is not very bright.

94. Text refers to the *printed word*. You can be talking about a small piece of language—a sentence or paragraph—or you might use the word to talk about an entire volume. Recently, the verb "to text" has entered our language. If you are younger than eighty, you know its meaning.

95. When something belongs to today's generation, we say that it is contemporary. Contemporary ads tend to contain very little text, whereas those of a previous generation are dense with text. In its noun form, a contemporary is someone who lives at the same time as another. You might say that Franklin Delano Roosevelt and Winston Churchill were contemporaries.

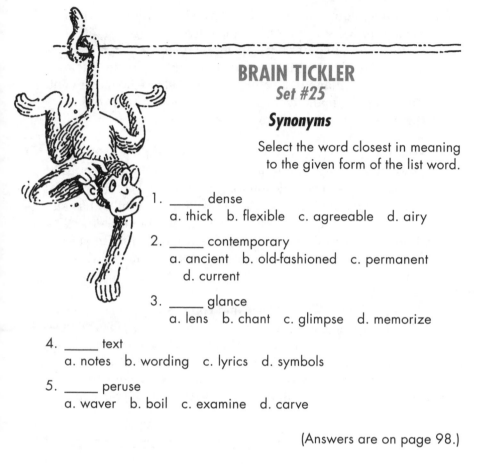

BRAIN TICKLER
Set #25

Synonyms

Select the word closest in meaning to the given form of the list word.

1. _____ dense
   a. thick   b. flexible   c. agreeable   d. airy

2. _____ contemporary
   a. ancient   b. old-fashioned   c. permanent
   d. current

3. _____ glance
   a. lens   b. chant   c. glimpse   d. memorize

4. _____ text
   a. notes   b. wording   c. lyrics   d. symbols

5. _____ peruse
   a. waver   b. boil   c. examine   d. carve

(Answers are on page 98.)

Meet Words 96 to 100!

96. Images are *visual pictures*. Sometimes they are actual visual pictures, such as those that might appear on the printed page. We also use images to refer to those pictures we can see in our minds—or, to put in another way, those we can imagine. A poem's effectiveness depends on its use of imagery.

97. To accelerate is to *speed up* or *increase*. A car that accelerates quickly has excellent pick-up. Going down a hill on your bike, you will not have any problem accelerating.

98. Maneuver comes from the Latin word *manuopera*, which means "to work by hand." To maneuver means to *move skillfully*. An expert chess player maneuvers his pieces across the board until his opponent must concede defeat. As a noun, a maneuver refers to such a strategic movement. For example, maneuvers served to position the troops in the perfect position for an attack.

99. Stability has two related meanings. The first has to do with physical stability. In this sense it means *strength, firmness,* and *balance*. Obviously you look for physical stability in houses and automobiles. The other kind of stability has an emotional flavor. It also refers to strength, but the emotional kind, the kind of stability one hopes to find in one's parents, for example. The adjective form of the word is stable, and the verb is stabilize.

100. If you've done something bad and you're sorry you've done it, what you're feeling is called remorse. Its word origin is interesting. Remorse comes from the Middle English word *remors* and the Latin word *remordere*. *Re-*, as you know, means "again," and *mors* (or *mordere*) means "to bite." So when you're remorseful, that awful feeling of *guilt* is biting you again.

BRAIN TICKLER
Set #26

Nuts or Not?

Read each sentence to decide if the underlined vocabulary word is used correctly in context. If the meaning is ludicrous, write "Nuts" in the blank space. If the sentence makes sense, write "Not" in the blank space.

1. _____ I was overcome with <u>remorse</u> when our team won the league championship and I was the hitting star of the game.

2. _____ Stuck on a steaming subway, Aaron filled his mind with <u>images</u> of iced tea and air conditioning.

3. _____ The first lesson for new drivers: when you come to a red light, <u>accelerate</u>.

4. _____ Mrs. Simpson is pleasant one day, vicious the next, and I admire her <u>stability</u>.

5. _____ In order to complete the obstacle course race, Oliver had to <u>maneuver</u> his way around three cones and two ditches.

(Answers are on page 98.)

Meet Words 101 to 105!

101. Adjacent means *near* or *next to*. Even though it's always an adjective, it can be used in two ways. You can say that the two adjacent buildings were both built in 1905. Often adjacent is paired with "to," as in "The two buildings built in 1905 are adjacent to each other."

102. When we say that a paragraph comprises, or *includes*, pieces of sentences, we mean that only pieces of sentences are included in that paragraph. Today most advertisements comprise (or contain) lots of images and little text.

103. Navigation is the practice or science of directing some traveling vehicle (a ship or aircraft, for example) or being from one place to its destination. In newer cars, a navigation system helps the driver find the correct route to wherever she's going.

104. If you possess an abundance of something, you have *a lot* of it. You have certainly seen the adjective form of the word—abundant—but you may be less familiar with the verb form, abound. You can say that this team abounds with superb athletes, which means an abundance of them comprise the team.

105. Leisure refers to free time and the activities we might choose to do in that time. It's very hard for most of us to imagine an era in which leisurely activities might include reading all the text in an ad.

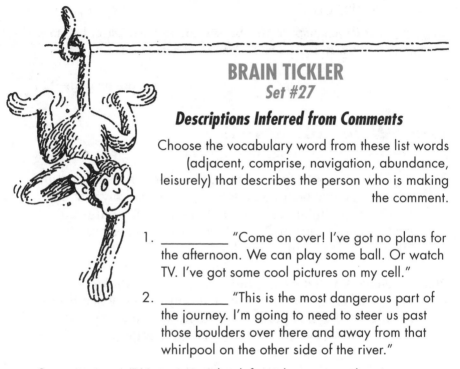

BRAIN TICKLER
Set #27

Descriptions Inferred from Comments

Choose the vocabulary word from these list words (adjacent, comprise, navigation, abundance, leisurely) that describes the person who is making the comment.

1. _____ "Come on over! I've got no plans for the afternoon. We can play some ball. Or watch TV. I've got some cool pictures on my cell."

2. _____ "This is the most dangerous part of the journey. I'm going to need to steer us past those boulders over there and away from that whirlpool on the other side of the river."

3. _____ "We just came back from the supermarket. Just open that refrigerator, and you'll see we can't fit another thing in there. It's filled with delicious food."

4. _____ "This photo is from the summer of 1996. There I am. On my right is Ted; on my left is Wendy."

5. _____ "These are my best qualities: I am kind to those in need of kindness, I try to be patient with everybody, and I listen carefully to what others say. These are the positive qualities that make up my personality."

(Answers are on page 98.)

IT'S NOT ONLY ABOUT LATIN

In this book you've learned that certain words have evolved from other words. "Mingle," you have learned, comes from Middle English, whereas "dignity" has Latin roots. It might be useful for you to know a little bit of the history of our language.

English belongs to a large family of languages, known as Indo-European. English is considered to be a Germanic language and is closest to the Frisian language, spoken today only in a region of the Netherlands. English is also related to German and Yiddish, but not as closely. Another major Indo-European group is the Romance languages, which includes Latin, Portuguese, Spanish, French, and Italian. As you have already seen, many words originally from Romance languages have entered the English language.

The history of the English language is divided into three periods: Old English, Middle English, and Modern English. Old English dates from 449 CE, when Germanic tribes invaded England. Old English is very different from the language we speak today. In fact, its alphabet includes some symbols you probably would not recognize. The Middle English period began in 1066 CE with the Norman Conquest, when French armies conquered England and brought with them their language. Although there had already been some Latin and Greek influence, at this time many more Romance words entered the English language.

You may have heard of the great Middle English poet, Geoffrey Chaucer, who wrote *The Canterbury Tales*. Were you to read the *Tales*, you would need a glossary for some help, but much of it would look familiar. Here's an example:

> A Knight ther was, and that a worthy man,
> That fro the time that he first bigan
> To riden out, he loved chivalrye,
> Trouthe and honour, freedom and curteisye.

Now that's not so difficult, is it?

The Modern English period begins about 1450. It is obviously a very comprehensive period, since it includes on one end the plays of Shakespeare and on the other the lyrics of Eminem.

BRAIN TICKLER
Set #28

Words in Context

Choose the correct form of the list word to complete the sentence. Look for context clues! The list words are: peruse, glance, dense, text, contemporary, images, accelerate, maneuver, stability, remorse, adjacent, comprise, navigation, abundance, and leisurely.

1. Chloe expresses her feelings of _____ for having lied to her parents, but her parents insisted that even one lie affects the trust they have enjoyed.

2. The movie screen was filled with dazzling _____ of underwater life.

3. Pablo Picasso and Henri Matisse were _____; even though they lived at the same time, they developed different styles of painting.

4. This year's eighth grade is a pleasure to teach, with a(n) _____ of hard-working, good-natured children.

5. The coffee shop is located across the street from the supermarket and _____ to the dry cleaners.

6. Just from his manners, I knew at first _____ that he was a kind, respectful child.

7. It's a mixed group, _____ athletically talented but unmotivated players.

8. If you don't know the answer to the question, simply return to the _____ and search for the appropriate passage.

9. With Captain Halladay at the controls, we _____ the chilly waters of the North Atlantic.

10. I hope you spend a(n) _____ summer, doing whatever you like . . . but not too much of any one thing.

11. Before you use that camera, it would be a good idea to _____ the manual and learn what you can about its operation.

12. The vehicle is known for its _____; in more than a dozen road tests, not one flipped over.

13. If you step on the gas too hard, the car will _____ too quickly.

14. Her camping gear was made of _____ material, which weighed her down and kept her from enjoying the hike.

15. It's a very exciting video game, which requires the skier to _____ through all kinds of dangerous obstacles.

(Answers are on page 98.)

ON YOUR OWN

Pretend you are an advertising executive from a bygone era. It's your job to fill the newspapers and magazines with an automobile ad that's big on text, but skimpy on images. Create a good paragraph or two that helps sell the vehicle. Use at least five list words from this chapter.

THE LAST WORD

Teachers mean well, but sometimes they hand out rules that apply in some situations, but certainly not in all. Here's one: don't begin a sentence with "because." Actually there's nothing wrong with that, as this example will demonstrate: Because we follow authority blindly, we lead ourselves into error. (This no-beginning-a-

sentence-with-"because" rule hopes to prevent sentence frag-
ments, like this: Because I am partial to Italian food.)

Do you remember learning about parts of speech? Do you
remember the "helpful" hint that adverbs often end with the -ly
suffix? Well, that lovely (hint!) rule is occasionally incorrect, as
"lovely" serves as an adjective in this case, modifying "rule." It
also applies to one of the list words from this chapter, "leisurely."
In some cases, it is an adverb: Can you imagine a world paced so
leisurely that readers would donate valuable time to an advertisement? ("Leisurely" modifies the verb "paced.") However, in
most cases, it's an adjective: She enjoyed a leisurely stroll
through the park.

Can you think of any other -ly words that are adjectives?

BRAIN TICKLERS—THE ANSWERS

Set #25, page 91

1. a
2. d
3. c
4. b
5. c

Set #26, page 92

1. nuts
2. not
3. nuts
4. nuts
5. not

Set #27, page 94

1. leisurely
2. maneuver
3. abundance
4. adjacent
5. comprise

Set #28, page 96

1. remorse
2. images
3. contemporaries
4. abundance
5. adjacent
6. glance
7. comprising
8. text
9. navigated
10. leisurely
11. peruse
12. stability
13. accelerate
14. dense
15. maneuver

CHAPTER EIGHT

Natural Disasters– Something Can Be Done

Electronic Dictionaries

In December 2004, a huge tsunami brought death and devastation to Southeast Asia. From Somalia to Thailand, children became orphans, and families were left homeless and destitute, unable to find food or lodging. The news media reported the awful consequences of the tsunami. Each night the evening news vividly broadcast them into our living rooms. As terrible as these events and their consequences may be, scientists warn us that they are, in a human sense, escalating.

While events of this kind cannot be prevented, measures can certainly be taken to minimize the damage they bring.

Natural disasters have not actually been increasing in number. What has happened is that the injury to humans has increased dramatically over the last century. In a way, technology is to blame, because technology has enabled people to live in areas that were not previously inhabitable. Poverty, too, must absorb some of the blame, because poor people have been pushed into some of these areas. That's where the problem lies: some of these areas are most susceptible to natural disasters.

Both the rich and poor seem willing to accept the risk. California real estate is among the most expensive in the world. The state's millions of residents have decided that the pleasures of West Coast life offset the danger of living along a fault line. At the other extreme are the poverty-stricken residents of Indonesia, who live within striking distance of that nation's 150 active volcanoes.

The difference between the rich and the poor lies not with the chances that disaster will strike—in such cases, natural disasters may be inevitable—but with how governments have responded to the challenge.

Take, for example, the Pacific Coast of the United States. In this area, governments have already upgraded construction codes for buildings and highways, creating flexible structures that will sway and not collapse. They have improved warning systems and done considerable research to determine the exact nature of the danger. Should disaster strike, structures are less likely to crumble, and people are more likely to survive.

That's not the case in poorer countries. Following a disaster, people are liable to return to where they have always lived, and buildings are more likely to be rebuilt in the exact same way.

Around the world, governments must develop policies that stress human disaster prevention. Governments cannot guarantee that natural disasters will not occur, but they certainly can offer some promise to try to save lives. The tsunami of 2004 and other disasters, like Hurricane Katrina in 2005, offered a very real reminder of how fragile human life is. The world should not need other reminders.

Meet Words 106 to 110!

106. Devastation is the noun form of the verb "to devastate," which comes from the Latin word *devastare*, "to lay waste." It should be easy to see why devastation means just about the same as *destruction*.

107. A person who is destitute is living without any of the necessities of life: a place to live, clean clothing, three square meals a day. It is a condition synonymous with homelessness.

108. Vividly is the adverb form of the adjective vivid, which has several closely related meanings. When we refer to vivid television images of tsunami destruction, we are thinking of *clear, detailed, colorful,* and maybe even *stunning* images. We can also think of an individual's personality as vivid, which means that person is *lively* and *bright*. A third sense is *strong* or *daring*, as in a vivid imagination.

109. What does an escalator do? Well, at least half the time, it brings you up. To escalate is to *rise*; in the late 1960s, the number of American troops in Vietnam escalated.

110. Enable is to give somebody the opportunity or the method to get something done. Technology enabled people to live in disaster-prone areas that perhaps were not meant for human habitation.

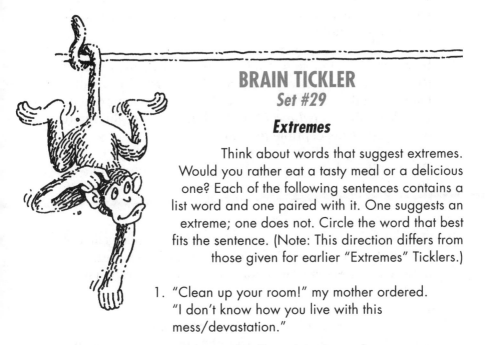

BRAIN TICKLER
Set #29

Extremes

Think about words that suggest extremes. Would you rather eat a tasty meal or a delicious one? Each of the following sentences contains a list word and one paired with it. One suggests an extreme; one does not. Circle the word that best fits the sentence. (Note: This direction differs from those given for earlier "Extremes" Ticklers.)

1. "Clean up your room!" my mother ordered. "I don't know how you live with this mess/devastation."

2. The Great Depression severely affected the lives of many Americans, leaving some destitute/uncomfortable.

3. His vivid/clear writing gave the reader insight into the dark beauty of the forest.

4. No one likes inflation, since it is almost certain to result in escalating/steady prices.

5. The teacher's guidance enabled/forced her students to complete their first literature essay.

(Answers are on page 110.)

Meet Words 111 to 115!

111. To inhabit a residence or area is to live or dwell in it. Therefore, that which is inhabitable is *suitable for living*. You wouldn't object to living in a mansion, but would you find a desert inhabitable?

112. If you are susceptible to colds, for example, you are likely to catch one or be affected by one. In a sense, the word means "easily taken advantage of." A serious runner might be susceptible or *vulnerable* to leg injuries. A slight, timid boy might be susceptible to bullies.

113. To offset is to *balance* or *make up for*. Judi doesn't like to study, but her superior intelligence offsets her so-so study habits.

114. That which is inevitable cannot be avoided. There's an old saying about the inevitability of death and taxes. Certain natural disasters are inevitable, but the human toll may not be.

115. To upgrade is to *improve*. Computer technology continually upgrades available features, thereby convincing consumers to purchase new ones every few years.

BRAIN TICKLER
Set #30

Words in Context

Use the correct forms of list words 111 to 115 (inhabitable, susceptible, offset, inevitable, upgrade) to complete this paragraph.

It is (1)_____ that appliances will grow old, and when they do, they become increasingly (2) _____ to all sorts of problems. The owner is then faced with a tough decision: should I repair what I already own, or should I purchase a(n) (3)_____? Repairs are costly, and purchasing a new one is even costlier, but these costs are (4)_____ by technological improvements and the pleasure of owning a brand-new product. You don't want to find yourself without an essential appliance. Let's face it: A home without a toaster or a microwave is practically (5) un_____.

(Answers are on page 110.)

Meet Words 116 to 120!

116. That which is flexible bends. It's *elastic*; it's *springy*. You might say this of a physical object, such as the cover of a paperback volume, or of a person, who can adapt to different kinds of demands and situations.

117. A system is a set of parts that work together as a whole. The digestive system, for example, consists of the mouth, the esophagus, the stomach, and the small intestines (among other organs), all working together to digest food. A system is also a *method* of doing something: Do you have a system for organizing your school papers?

118. Liable means *likely*. If you are liable to, say, score a high grade on a science test, then that is the probable outcome. In another sense (a legal one), the word means *obligated*.

119. A policy is a method or rule chosen to guide present and future decisions. For example, your school district may have a dress policy that tells students what they may and may not wear to school.

120. Something that is fragile is liable to break. Just as "flexible" may refer to humans and non-humans, so may "fragile." You may say that a glass vase is fragile, and you may say that a person is fragile because that individual's feelings are easily hurt.

BRAIN TICKLER
Set #31

Antonyms

Select the word nearly opposite in meaning to the list word. Keep in mind that some of the list words may be presented in different word forms. There will be one left over.

_____ 1. flexible   a. sturdy

_____ 2. systematic   b. unlikely

_____ 3. liable   c. rigid

_____ 4. policy   d. spontaneity

_____ 5. fragile   e. costly

                                f. disorganized

(Answers are on page 110.)

ELECTRONIC DICTIONARIES

Chances are you have regular access to a computer, and if you do, you're in luck. Online dictionaries can do just about anything regular dictionaries do, and they may be absolutely free.

Here's all you need to do.

Using your Web browser, type in "online dictionaries," and you'll be presented with a wide range of choices. Some of the hardcover dictionaries that you may be familiar with (Merriam-Webster, for example) maintain their own online dictionaries, too, and they're great. Some companies (Bartleby's, for example) have developed online dictionaries, which are just as good, just as comprehensive.

Once you find one you like using, just add it to your list of Web site "favorites," and you'll have easy access to it.

These Web sites offer multiple resources (thesauruses, encyclopedias, and quotation guides, to name a few), and you will need to determine which are free of charge and which require some membership fee.

Naturally, you can always purchase a dictionary program in CD form and load that on your hard drive. Because of the availability of online dictionaries, these programs are no longer pricey.

Nowadays, given the size and portable nature of computers, you never need to be without a dictionary! One can fit easily in your shirt pocket.

BRAIN TICKLER
Set #32

Words in Context

Choose the correct form of the list word to complete the sentence. Look for context clues! The list words are: devastation, destitute, vivid, escalate, enable, inhabitable, susceptible, offset, inevitable, upgrade, flexible, system, liable, policy, and fragile.

1. The company's _____ prevents workers from working part-time for its competitors.

2. "With a fresh coat of paint," my father said, "this apartment will again be _____."

3. Serena's vision had gotten very weak, but audio books _____ her to listen to the novels she once would have read.

4. Despite everyone's best efforts to help every student pass, every year it is _____ that a small group of students fail and must attend summer school.

5. "The wrist is still a tiny bit _____," the doctor said, removing the cast, "so try not to play any contact sports for a couple of weeks."

6. The hurricane left unimaginable _____ in its wake: thousands of homes and businesses were destroyed by the powerful wind and rain.

7. This camera is the best I've ever owned. Just look at these pictures. Can you believe how _____ they are?

8. The salesman asked about the car I was presently driving and then suggested that I _____ to a newer, fancier model.

9. Because Tina had always taken for granted the comforts of home and family, she could not imagine what it would be like to be _____ for even a little while.

10. Our school installed a new computer _____, which has made it easier for teachers and students to use the Internet.

11. "I'm _____ in terms of tonight's plans," Ray said. "The movies sound good, but I'm O.K. with just hanging out, too."

12. The general reported that, with the enemy's advance, he would need to _____ the number of troops and weapons on the ground.

13. Keeping the thermostat too high dries out your nasal passages and leaves you very _____ to winter colds.

14. The profit that we realized from the sale of our old home more than _____ the cost of moving to our new one.

15. "If you don't get that inspection sticker taken care of," my neighbor warned, "you're _____ to get a summons."

(Answers are on page 110.)

ON YOUR OWN

Go online and get some information about a natural disaster that was surprisingly visible—and vivid—to the American public: the California earthquake of October 1989. From your research, record in note form some interesting information about this natural disaster. Be sure to use at least five words from this chapter.

- _____

_____

- _____

_____

- _____

_____

- _____

_____

- _____

_____

THE LAST WORD

Since you are now familiar with the word devastation, you can probably guess the meaning of the verb form, "to devastate": to lay waste or to destroy. It sounds like a serious word, right? Well, originally (and for a long time), it was serious, but lately it's taken on some less serious shades of meaning. You could say, for example, that the devastating (adjective form) pass rush of the New England Patriots decided the Super Bowl. Yes, the Patriots' linemen may have had their way with the opposition, but the outcome was a lot less serious than the destruction an earthquake might bring. Strangely, the word sometimes has a positive connotation: you might say that the band's performance was just devastating. In that case, you heartily approve.

BRAIN TICKLERS—THE ANSWERS

Set #29, page 103

1. mess
2. destitute
3. vivid
4. escalating
5. enabled

Set #30, page 105

1. inevitable
2. susceptible
3. upgrade
4. offset
5. inhabitable

Set #31, page 106

1. c
2. f
3. b

4. d
5. a

Set #32, page 108

1. policy
2. inhabitable
3. enabled
4. inevitable
5. fragile
6. devastation
7. vivid
8. upgrade
9. destitute
10. system
11. flexible
12. escalate
13. susceptible
14. offset
15. liable

CHAPTER NINE

The Middle School Years— How Much Do They Matter?

Using a Thesaurus

As the school year wanes, many eighth graders take note of a fact that earlier may not have been obvious: from here on in, everything counts.

It is not hard to comprehend the truth of that statement. From now on, grades appear on high school records. High school records (not to mention test scores) lead to college acceptance letters. The caliber of college one attends determines the extent to which one will succeed in life. It sounds kind of ominous, doesn't it? You wouldn't mind crawling back under the covers, right?

Seen from this narrow perspective—as merely a summary of grades earned—the middle school years might not look like much. In this limited sense, middle school simply ends when high school begins. Out of sight, out of mind, right?

But there are a few ways in which middle school matters very much. This is something the alert, conscientious middle school student has always known.

For most students, academic success is not something that can be turned on and off like a faucet. The study habits one brings to high school and beyond were formed during the previous thirteen or fourteen years. As the word "habit" suggests, learning to be an excellent student is largely a matter of practice, of establishing and repeating study routines that lead to success.

Skills are of paramount importance in the middle school years. Both middle and high school teachers are concerned, of course, with content, as well as with skills. However, in middle school, the primary focus is on skill building. In order for students to be able to assimilate the content of high school courses, they must first acquire a set of essential skills. They must, for example, be good readers, but they must also be taught to think while they read. A skilled middle school reader will discern, for example, a writer's purpose, while a merely adequate reader cannot. A student who comes to high school lacking these essential skills will have a hard time trying to fill in the gaps.

Finally, middle school is a great time for trying things out. It's a great time for adopting a risk-taking attitude, for losing that cautious old self who may have cared too much about winning, losing, and public opinion. You'd like to be a member of the debate club? Check it out. You wanted to try your hand at lacrosse? Hey, why not? You wondered if musicals might be your thing? Go and find out. There's no time like the present.

Here's the long and short of it: Anyone who thinks middle school doesn't count has probably missed out on a great opportunity. There's nothing that counts more than opportunities that won't come again.

Meet Words 121 to 125!

121. To wane is to *become smaller* or to *fade*. The school year probably starts to wane big-time around mid-May. If you see your savings wane, it's probably time to cut back on the expenses.

122. Reading comprehension is the ability to make sense of what you are reading. If you comprehend material that's been introduced in class, then you *understand* it. It comes from a word that means to grasp or seize. You can see the connection.

123. Caliber refers to a particular *quality* or *level*. If you possess superior credentials, you can count on attending a college of a higher caliber.

124. Extent sounds a lot like "extend," which means to stretch, and extent is the degree to which a thing can stretch. It refers to a certain *size* or *amount*. It can refer to the *limit* to which something can go, as in the extent of the law.

125. That which is ominous is *threatening*. The idea that school suddenly counts in a whole new way might strike you as ominous. Some people feel that a jury's refusing to look directly at a defendant is an ominous sign.

BRAIN TICKLER
Set #33

Nuts or Not?

Read each sentence to decide if the underlined vocabulary word is used correctly in context. If the meaning is ludicrous, write "Nuts" in the blank space. If the sentence makes sense, write "Not" in the blank space.

1. _____ Before I can form an opinion about what the professor is saying, I need to <u>comprehend</u> her main points.

2. _____ Denise's hopes of gaining a victory began to <u>wane</u> when the team fell behind by twenty points.

3. _____ If you really want to see theater of the very best <u>caliber</u>, you ought to come to New York.

4. _____ I was absolutely starving, so the sight of eggs, sausage, potatoes, and toast was especially <u>ominous</u>.

5. _____ Your grade in this class depends on the <u>extent</u> to which you are willing to work.

(Answers are on page 124.)

Meet Words 126 to 130!

126. Perspective is like *point of view*, the position from which one sees something. If you're thinking of middle school as an experience that doesn't matter, then that's your perspective on middle school. In art, perspective refers to the way things are drawn in order to show the way they appear to the eye.

127. When you say that a perspective is limited, you mean that the viewer wishes to limit, or restrict, what he sees. Entrance to a ride at the amusement park may be limited, or *restricted*, to persons of a certain height.

128. Certainly you know people who are conscientious about their work or their behavior in general. To most of us, this word has many positive connotations. It suggests a person who is *careful, thorough*, and willing to work hard. In effect, it describes a person who is willing to listen to his or her conscience.

129. To establish is to *create* or *set up*. Good students soon learn to establish effective study routines. Governments establish laws that protect the rights of citizens. ("Establish" shares the same root as one of the words from Chapter Seven. Can you find it?)

130. Paramount means *chief*—first and foremost. Of course middle schools are concerned with facts and knowledge, but their paramount objective is skill development. In baseball, hitting, fielding, and running are all keys to success, but good pitching is paramount.

BRAIN TICKLER
Set #34

Descriptions Inferred from Actions

Choose the vocabulary word (perspective, limited, conscientious, establish, paramount) that describes the person, animal, or thing that is mentioned.

1. _____ Whenever Kristin knows she has a test, she gathers her notes, books, and homework and sets aside plenty of time to study.

2. _____ Tom works hard, he's active in the community, and he keeps in touch with his friends, but what's easily most important to him is his family.

3. _____ Jack's taste in food runs strictly to American fare; he won't even try ethnic foods.

4. _____ The painter positioned herself in the clearing across the road so that she would have an excellent view of the church she wished to paint.

5. _____ Betty Friedan founded the National Organization for Women in order to create a group that would fight for women's rights.

(Answers are on page 124.)

Meet Words 131 to 135!

131. When we refer to the content of a book or a course, we are talking about the *subject matter*. Sometimes the plural noun will be used. You could say that you checked the contents printed on the side of the cereal box because you wanted to know how much sugar the cereal contained.

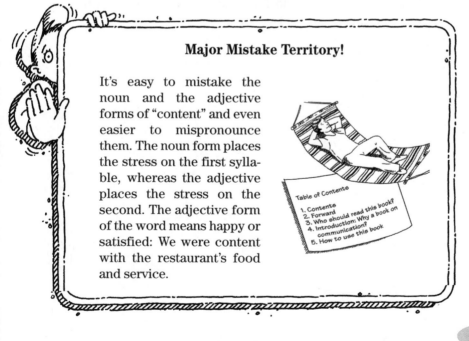

Major Mistake Territory!

It's easy to mistake the noun and the adjective forms of "content" and even easier to mispronounce them. The noun form places the stress on the first syllable, whereas the adjective places the stress on the second. The adjective form of the word means happy or satisfied: We were content with the restaurant's food and service.

Table of Contents

1. Contents
2. Forward
3. Who should read this book?
4. Introduction: Why a book on communication?
5. How to use this book

132. To assimilate means to *take in* and *absorb*. The introductory essay talks about students assimilating the content of the course, which means they take it in and learn it. In other sense, assimilate means to *fit in*. We often use this word to describe people of one culture who want to fit into another. Immigrants to America wish to assimilate, but they also hope to keep some of their own ethnic identity.

133. A few years ago there was a coffee commercial that boasted that its product was only for the most discerning. To discern is to be able to *tell the difference* between one thing and another. It can also mean to *detect*, as in the introductory essay, which says that a good middle school reader can discern elements that a lesser reader cannot.

134. You are probably familiar with one specialized meaning of adopt: to take responsibility for a child. Many Westerners wished to adopt children who lost their parents to the 2004 tsunami. In a more general sense, it means to *take on* or to *accept*. As a middle schooler, the attitude you adopt will make a great difference in your experience of middle school.

135. You can't get into a car without seeing a caution sign, which means that the driver needs to check things out before proceeding. Cautious describes such a person or act: it means just about the same as *careful*.

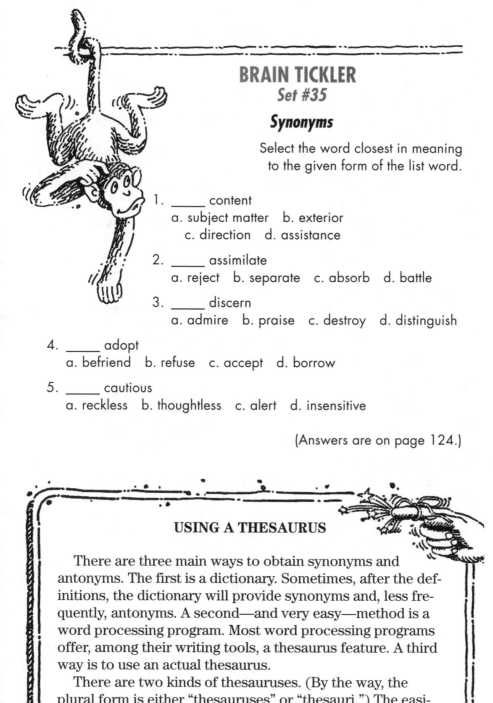

BRAIN TICKLER
Set #35

Synonyms

Select the word closest in meaning to the given form of the list word.

1. _____ content
   a. subject matter b. exterior
      c. direction d. assistance

2. _____ assimilate
   a. reject b. separate c. absorb d. battle

3. _____ discern
   a. admire b. praise c. destroy d. distinguish

4. _____ adopt
   a. befriend b. refuse c. accept d. borrow

5. _____ cautious
   a. reckless b. thoughtless c. alert d. insensitive

(Answers are on page 124.)

USING A THESAURUS

There are three main ways to obtain synonyms and antonyms. The first is a dictionary. Sometimes, after the definitions, the dictionary will provide synonyms and, less frequently, antonyms. A second—and very easy—method is a word processing program. Most word processing programs offer, among their writing tools, a thesaurus feature. A third way is to use an actual thesaurus.

There are two kinds of thesauruses. (By the way, the plural form is either "thesauruses" or "thesauri.") The easiest thesaurus to use is a simple dictionary of synonyms and antonyms. It is arranged in alphabetical order, and after each word the reader can easily locate words of similar or opposite meaning.

More advanced language lovers may wish to avail themselves of a standard thesaurus, such as *Roget's Thesaurus*. (Dr. Peter Mark Roget organized and compiled the first thesaurus of this kind.)

Let's say you wish to find synonyms and antonyms for the word "ominous." You begin your search by turning to the back of the book, an index arranged in alphabetical order. There you will find several meanings for "ominous"—among these is "threatening"—and next to each meaning is a number. The number next to "threatening" is 514.3.

The first part of a standard thesaurus is arranged numerically, so to find synonyms for "ominous"/"threatening," you have to locate section 514.3. (One of the cool features of a standard thesaurus is the fact that it doesn't have page numbers!) You will find that topic number 514 is "THREAT," and if you look under sub-category 3, you will see a host of synonyms—all adjectives—for "ominous": "threatening," "menacing," and so forth.

So how can you find an antonym? Well, this strategy works sometimes, but not always. Look at the topic that precedes or follows. In this case, topic number 513 is "CURSE," and 515 is "FASTING." Hmm, neither sounds promising, right?

So your next move is to look back at 514.3 and you'll see other numbers given to you, including 133.17 for "foreboding." Once you locate that topic ("PREMONITION"), you will see that 133.18 offers a bunch of useful antonyms: "auspicious," "favorable," "promising," and others.

Of course, you may not be certain which of these is the most precise antonym, and that uncertainty might send you back to a dictionary.

BRAIN TICKLER
Set #36

Words in Context

Choose the correct form of the list word to complete the sentence. Look for context clues! The list words are: wane, comprehend, caliber, extent, ominous, perspective, limited, conscientious, establish, paramount, content, assimilate, discern, adopt, and cautious.

1. To me, one cola tastes pretty much like another. It's impossible for me to _____ the difference between Pepsi and Coke.

2. The district attorney promised to pursue the case to the fullest _____ of the law.

3. Phil tends to be _____ when he walks through the woods, because he just isn't confident of his footing on the forest trails.

4. I thought the first *Star Wars* film was sensational, but they got old in a hurry and with each one my enthusiasm _____.

5. Ursula was extremely _____ about her taxes. She kept records of every expense and every possible deduction.

6. The school's _____ concern was to increase attendance, which explains why the secretaries called home whenever a student missed even one day.

7. The lecturer provided us with a great deal of information about World War I; in order to _____ all this material, I had to look over my notes a few times.

8. Our trip to Spain was wonderful, but it would have been even better had I been able to _____ a single word of Spanish.

9. In the 1960s, both Russia and the United States hoped to become the first nation to _____ a presence in outer space.

10. A basketball player of his astonishing _____ is sure to be taken in the first round of the draft.

11. From George Washington's _____, the Revolutionary War was a struggle of men fighting for their freedom; Britain's King George III undoubtedly saw things differently.

12. The sky seemed about to burst, and I feared these _____ weather conditions would spoil our picnic plans.

13. When a cat purrs, you know it is _____.

14. Brandon is such a follower; as soon as he sees something cool, he's sure to _____ it as his own.

15. Because of Matthew's _____ understanding of calculus, he had to take an extra math course.

(Answers are on page 124.)

ON YOUR OWN

Does the introductory essay connect with your own experience of middle school? How do/did you feel about middle school? Did you squeeze every drop from it? Or were you the kind who didn't give it your all because you sensed it just didn't count? Write a personal response to the introductory essay, and be sure to use at least five list words from this chapter.

THE LAST WORD

That which is ominous serves as an omen. What's an omen? Well, in the ancient world, omens were found in nature. The flight of birds or a thunderclap could be a sign that the gods were smiling or frowning on earthly events. Omens, you might say, evolved into what we now call superstitions. Seeing a black cat, walking under a ladder, and breaking a mirror are signs of trouble headed one's way.

What's interesting here is that omens could be positive or negative. So why is it that ominous almost always has a negative connotation?

BRAIN TICKLERS—THE ANSWERS

Set #33, page 115

1. not
2. not
3. not
4. nuts
5. not

Set #34, page 116

1. conscientious
2. paramount
3. limited
4. perspective
5. establish

Set #35, page 119

1. a
2. c
3. d
4. c
5. c

Set #36, page 121

1. discern
2. extent
3. cautious
4. waned
5. conscientious
6. paramount
7. assimilate
8. comprehend
9. establish
10. caliber
11. perspective
12. ominous
13. content
14. adopt
15. limited

CHAPTER TEN

Bargain Hunters–Going to Unreasonable Lengths

New Words Through Technology

People generally feel pretty pleased with themselves when they've paid less for something. You've seen that smug expression on people's faces when they tell you they paid less than you did: "Well, I only paid $19.99 for that same shirt." You've paid twice that, so you might resent them a little. Nevertheless, you feign admiration. "That's a great price," you admit. "You got yourself some deal there."

You walk away muttering to yourself, "What's wrong with people? Are we obsessed with this unending quest for bargains?"

There's nothing wrong with keeping a little extra change in your pocket instead of the pockets of the merchants. But sometimes you have to wonder if we don't overdo it.

Here's a situation you might be familiar with: it's the "time-is-money" dilemma. Let's say some potential patron is looking for an alarm clock, a common, everyday item. In his search for the best price for that clock, this customer visits three stores in three different shopping malls in three different neighborhoods. Yes, in the end, he might end up saving a few dollars, but what about the fuel costs and the parking fees and the expensive lunch he consumed in the second mall? What about the three hours that are now lost? Can a price be put on those? Think of it this way: a truly industrious person might have lost three hours of salary.

Then there's the case of buying more than you need. This actually falls within two categories. Have you ever seen those sales where you have to buy a large quantity of, say, cans of tuna in order to get the sale price? Well, the problem there is that you might not use all of those cans before their expiration date. Or you might not wish to allocate an entire shelf to storing all those cans. The second category involves purchasing an enormous portion in order to get the sale price. You might have to buy a huge box of breakfast cereal, enough to feed your family for six months. That's not necessarily such a bad idea, but you know what happens. Your family gets tired of eating the same cereal day after day, and this huge cereal box just sits forever on the shelf. Eventually you get sick of looking at it, and you discard it. Or the cereal grows stale, a distinct possibility.

Merchants offer sales in order to convince you to buy more than you really need. Someone once said to Mr. Heinz, "I bet you've made a lot of money from the ketchup people have eaten." Mr. Heinz corrected his questioner: "Actually, I've made a lot of money from the ketchup people have left on their plates."

If you've ever poured ketchup on your fries, you know there's nothing subtle about Mr. Heinz's point. Next time you go shopping, try to remember the old saying you might have heard from your parents: "Your eyes are bigger than your stomach."

Meet Words 136 to 140!

136. A long time ago, smug meant "neat" or "trim," but, as you can tell from the introductory essay, its meaning has changed. Now it means *self-satisfied* . . . too self-satisfied.

137. To resent is to feel or show displeasure with another's behavior or words. When someone reminds you that he paid less than you did for, say, an item of clothing, you might resent or *dislike* his bringing that to your attention.

138. Feign has a couple of meanings. The first is to make up or *invent* a story or an excuse. The second, the one used in this passage, is to *pretend* or make a false show. You may be familiar with the noun form of the word—feint—which means an intentionally misleading move, such as a fencer might perform.

139. To mutter is to *mumble* or say something under your breath, usually if you're annoyed with someone or something and you don't want the rest of the world to know the full extent of your displeasure.

140. A quest is a *search* for something. Sometimes it's a long search that comes with all sorts of dangers. You may have heard of Jason and the Argonauts and their quest for the Golden Fleece.

BRAIN TICKLER
Set #37

Descriptions Inferred from Comments

Choose the vocabulary word from these list words (resentful, smug, on a quest, feigning, muttering) that describes the person who is making the comment.

1. _____ "I have searched high and low for an original Instamatic camera, but they are almost impossible to find."

2. _____ "I can't stand that Willie. He thinks he's the greatest thing since sliced bread. Did you see him look my way when Mrs. Wheldon returned the test papers? And to think he beat me by one measly point!"

3. _____ "This is the best strategy: Just pretend that you're interested. Keep nodding your head. Ask a few questions. It works like a gem."

4. _____ "I stood on that platform waiting twenty minutes for the train to arrive. One finally came, but it was packed, and I couldn't get on. When that train closed its doors, I had some choice words for it."

5. _____ "When I finished first in the 800 meter event, a smile crept onto my face. I was just so pleased with myself, I couldn't help but show it."

(Answers are on page 136.)

Meet Words 141 to 145!

141. A merchant is someone who buys and sells goods for profit. When you think of a merchant, you tend to think of someone who owns a store. On the streets of big cities, you might find merchants selling their goods, or merchandise.

142. A dilemma is a *problem* that doesn't have an obvious solution. It's kind of a no-win situation. Searching for the best bargain can be a dilemma because you're using extra time, which is itself worth a great deal.

143. Potential can be used as a noun or an adjective. When you say that a student displays a lot of potential, you're saying that she's got a lot of *promise* or *aptitude*. In the introductory essay, it's used as an adjective: a potential patron is a person who is likely to become a patron.

144. Patron has two meanings. The first is a *supporter* of some cause. A person could be a patron of the arts, which means that person donates money or support of some other kind. A more general meaning is the one used in the passage. A patron in that sense is a *client*, someone who might be purchasing goods or services.

145. To consume is to *eat* or to *use up* in some other way. You can consume a hearty lunch, or you can say that searching for a bargain managed to consume most of your afternoon. In another sense, we say that someone is consumed by, say, a hunger for bargains. We mean that this interest in bargains borders on obsession.

BRAIN TICKLER
Set #38

Words in Context

Use the correct forms of list words 141 to 145 (merchant, dilemma, potential, patron, consumed) to complete this paragraph.

Every time a(n) (1)_____ thinks about making a purchase, he or she faces a bit of a(n) (2) _____: Does the (3) _____ joy that this purchase will bring me offset the price I will have to pay? Were the object something like a delicious slice of pizza, something that could be (4) _____ and enjoyed immediately, the decision would not be so difficult. The joy would be great, and who would care about the relatively small amount spent? Usually, however, the decision is not so clear-cut, and it is up to the (5) _____ to convince the customer that the price is not as great as it seems and the joy far greater.

(Answers are on page 136.)

Meet Words 146 to 150!

146. An industrious person displays the quality of—you guessed it—industry, which is to say that this person is *hard-working*, conscientious, and likes to keep busy.

147. To allocate is to *assign* or *distribute*. No one has unlimited storage space, right? So you might not wish to allocate an entire shelf to the cans you had to purchase in order to take advantage of a sale.

148. When you discard something, you simply get rid of it: paper wrappers, a playing card you don't need, an expired coupon, a worn-out pair of jeans (just kidding—who discards worn jeans?).

149. When you say that something is distinct, you're saying that it's clearly *different* from others of its kind. If the superiority of the New England Patriots' defense is distinct, that means it is apparent to everyone.

150. Subtle suggests a *slight* difference, one that can be difficult to discern. There may be nothing subtle about the stylistic difference between Shakespeare's *Romeo and Juliet* and S. E. Hinton's *The Outsiders*, right? However, the difference between Coke and Pepsi could be subtle, especially for a person who doesn't drink colas. (By the way, don't pronounce the "b"; it sounds like "suttle." A subtle person is *clever* enough to get the difference.)

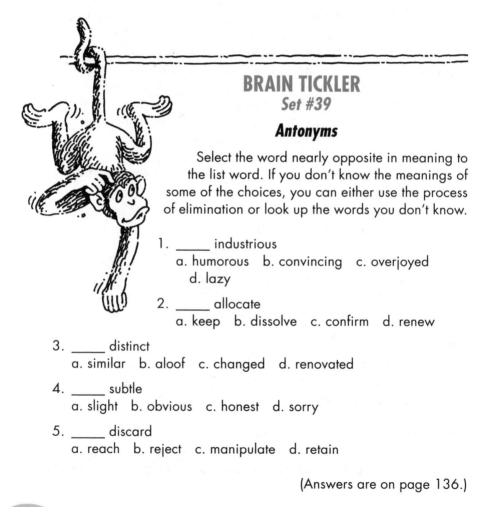

BRAIN TICKLER
Set #39

Antonyms

Select the word nearly opposite in meaning to the list word. If you don't know the meanings of some of the choices, you can either use the process of elimination or look up the words you don't know.

1. _____ industrious
   a. humorous   b. convincing   c. overjoyed
   d. lazy

2. _____ allocate
   a. keep   b. dissolve   c. confirm   d. renew

3. _____ distinct
   a. similar   b. aloof   c. changed   d. renovated

4. _____ subtle
   a. slight   b. obvious   c. honest   d. sorry

5. _____ discard
   a. reach   b. reject   c. manipulate   d. retain

(Answers are on page 136.)

WOULD YOU PLEASE
XEROX THAT DOCUMENT?

The English language does not stand still. It is always changing.

Words that once held meaning for speakers sometimes fall into disuse and may disappear from the language altogether. A more common event, however, is its opposite: words enter the language, and the language grows.

As you know, technology and the marketplace work together. Companies invent new products, and consumers are willing to pay for them. Whenever a new product comes into being, a new word often accompanies it.

That was certainly the case with Xerox copiers. The Xerox Corporation invented a very handy way of duplicating documents: the Xerox copier. Obviously, it was a big hit with consumers. Before long, the word "Xerox" came to represent not only a large corporation, but also the name of an increasingly popular duplicating machine. In fact, the word "Xerox" became so embedded in the public vocabulary that a duplicating machine manufactured by another company might very well be called a Xerox machine. Eventually the word "Xerox" became synonymous with "copier," and the verb "to xerox" came to mean "to duplicate."

Think about it: ten years ago, who had ever heard of an iPod?

BRAIN TICKLER
Set #40
Words in Context

Choose the correct form of the list word to complete the sentence. Look for context clues! The list words are: smug, resent, feign, mutter, quest, merchant, dilemma, potential, patron, consume, industrious, allocate, discard, distinct, and subtle.

1. I really didn't know very much about stopwatches, but the _____ was very helpful in explaining to me their different features.

2. This year's budget doesn't _____ as much as we'd like for repairing the physical plant.

3. Every time Tim scores a basket, you can see that _____ look creep onto his face.

4. Howard was a very successful student in elementary school, so we can conclude that he has the _____ to become an equally successful middle school student.

5. I knew exactly what my mother had gotten me for my birthday, but I thought it was an excellent idea to _____ surprise, anyway.

6. How many hamburgers can you _____ in one sitting? My record is four!

7. The waitress was unhappy with the tip we'd left her, and I could hear her _____ something unpleasant as she left our table.

8. There is nothing _____ about New York City: Its sights, its sounds, even its smells all inform you that you couldn't be anywhere else.

9. Of course I expect you to _____ your gum wrapper, but I don't want you to throw it out the car window.

10. Theresa faced a(n) _____ when the school year began, because she didn't know whether she wanted to play soccer or track, both offered in the same sports cycle.

11. I don't _____ Zina's success; I just wish she were a little less obnoxious about it.

12. By contributing generously year after year, Mrs. Andrews became a(n) _____ of the museum.

13. Kenny believed there was a(n) _____ difference between fresh-brewed coffee, which he loved, and instant coffee, which he despised.

14. When it came to shoes, Carol knew exactly what she wanted, and she gladly embarked upon a(n) _____ to find the right pair.

15. It would be hard to imagine a more _____ worker than Peter, who arrived early, stayed late, and even worked through lunch.

(Answers are on page 136.)

ON YOUR OWN

Look around your room—or your home or your school. Find a product that came into use recently (you decide what "recently" means). Do some research about the development and use of that product, and write a good body paragraph about it. Be sure to use at least five list words from this chapter.

THE LAST WORD

Are you familiar with the term onomatopoeia? Yes, it's a mouthful. Here's how you pronounce it: ah'-no-ma'-to-pe'-uh. It's a literary term used to categorize a word that sounds like what it is. Robert Frost's famous poem "Out, Out—" begins with this first line:

The buzz-saw snarled and rattled in the yard

The line contains several examples of onomatopoeia, including the word "buzz-saw," which sounds a lot like what buzz-saws do. The same can be said of "snarled" and "rattled."

One of our list words for this chapter is an example of onomatopoeia. Can you find it?

BRAIN TICKLERS—THE ANSWERS

Set #37, page 129

1. on a quest
2. resentful
3. feigning
4. muttering
5. smug

Set #38, page 131

1. patron
2. dilemma
3. potential
4. consumed
5. merchant

Set #39, page 132

1. d
2. a
3. a
4. b
5. d

Set #40, page 134

1. merchant
2. allocate
3. smug
4. potential
5. feign
6. consume
7. mutter
8. subtle
9. discard
10. dilemma
11. resent
12. patron
13. distinct
14. quest
15. industrious

CHAPTER ELEVEN

The Phone Keeps Ringing
The Verbal Analogy Bridge

After a grueling day at the office, I feel I have the right to an evening of serenity when I finally make it home. After all, a man's home is his palace, right?

Well, not exactly.

The problem is the multitude of solicitors who, it seems, have resolved to interrupt every task I am determined to complete. And what are these tasks? Nothing spectacular, I assure you: simply those monotonous, though enjoyable, pursuits that conclude a day. You know: things like dinner and doing the dishes and catching up on a little e-mail and TV.

Here's a typical interruption: the phone call from a charitable organization.

First, the caller identifies the organization. It takes me just a moment to infer his true purpose from his tone and content. He wants some of my money. Then he goes on to remind me of the benevolent work his organization performs. I don't need reminding. I know the compassionate nature of the organization's work. That's why I've contributed each of the last five years. What I really need is for the phone call to come to an end so that I can resume preparing dinner. But that doesn't happen as soon as I'd like. The caller thanks me for having contributed in the past, but he wants to know if this year I'll be willing to take the next step and donate as much as $500. So I brashly take control of the conversation. I tell him that I will contribute $50, precisely what I gave last year.

That's when he really starts to annoy me. He wonders if $250 would be possible. I say no. Well, how about $200? No. In this manner, the amount of the request gradually dwindles, until we settle upon the $50 I've always given.

I don't get it. What makes him think I've had such a terrific year that I'd go from $50 to $500? And why does he have to make me feel like a miser because $50 is all I can afford?

By the time I return to chopping vegetables, not only am I $50 poorer, I have also given up any hope of a quiet peaceful evening. After all, it's only 6:30, lots of time for the phone to keep ringing.

Meet Words 151 to 155!

151. A grueling (pronounced "grooling") experience is one that takes a lot out of you. Lots of adults have jobs that they find grueling, *demanding*, or *exhausting*. If you had to endure three exams in the same day, you'd probably find that grueling, too.

152. After a grueling day, you'd enjoy some portion of serenity, a period of *calm* and *quiet* during which you might listen to some relaxing music or swap e-mails with friends. The adjective form of the word is "serene."

153. Multitude refers to a large number—a never-ending stream of phone calls, in this case, but you could also complain about a multitude of pop-ups or homework assignments or annoying siblings.

154. A solicitor is one who solicits, one who asks or begs for one thing or another. Telephone solicitors often ask for contributions, but you might solicit some help with homework or some social advice.

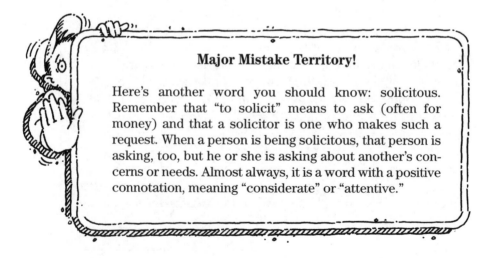

Major Mistake Territory!

Here's another word you should know: solicitous. Remember that "to solicit" means to ask (often for money) and that a solicitor is one who makes such a request. When a person is being solicitous, that person is asking, too, but he or she is asking about another's concerns or needs. Almost always, it is a word with a positive connotation, meaning "considerate" or "attentive."

155. Resolve is one of those words that can be a noun or a verb. If you resolve (verb) to get in shape, you make up your mind to exercise and eat well, but you know that doing so will require plenty of resolve (noun) or *determination*.

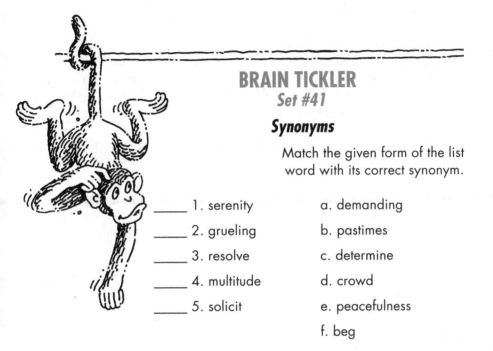

BRAIN TICKLER
Set #41

Synonyms

Match the given form of the list word with its correct synonym.

_____ 1. serenity

_____ 2. grueling

_____ 3. resolve

_____ 4. multitude

_____ 5. solicit

a. demanding

b. pastimes

c. determine

d. crowd

e. peacefulness

f. beg

(Answers are on page 148.)

Meet Words 156 to 160!

156. To assure is to *guarantee*. I assure you that this is the correct definition. The expression "self-assured" has a different meaning. It refers to confidence in one's abilities.

157. A monotonous experience is one that is *repetitive* and *boring*. Do you ever call someone and get a busy signal? Is that monotonous, or what?

158. To pursue means to follow. Its noun form, *pursuit*, refers either to the *search* itself or the *goal* of that search. For example, the narrator's pursuit of a peaceful evening is often ended by unwanted phone calls. These phone calls keep him from enjoying an evening of more pleasurable pursuits.

159. Conclude has two basic meanings. In The Phone Keeps Ringing the narrator refers to those activities that con-clude—or *end*—a day. You will see this same sense of the word in the "conclusion" of a novel. But conclude can also refer to a thought process, the one by which you come to your own conclusion. For example, you may certainly conclude that the narrator does not appreciate telephone solicitors.

160. That brings us to infer. This word means just about the same as the second meaning of *conclude*. If you infer from this example that English has lots of words with similar meanings, you are 100% correct.

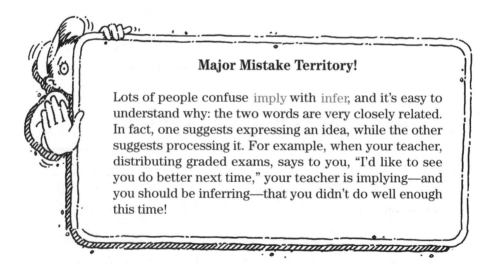

Major Mistake Territory!

Lots of people confuse imply with infer, and it's easy to understand why: the two words are very closely related. In fact, one suggests expressing an idea, while the other suggests processing it. For example, when your teacher, distributing graded exams, says to you, "I'd like to see you do better next time," your teacher is implying—and you should be inferring—that you didn't do well enough this time!

BRAIN TICKLER
Set #42

Words in Context

Write the correct list word (conclude, infer, assure, monotonous, pursuit) in the appropriate space.

Some critics of rap music claim that the lyrics are hateful and the melodies (1) _____, but any serious student of rap can (2) _____ these critics that this is not the case. Admirers of rap will argue that rap artists are as serious in their chosen (3) _____ as are today's poets and writers. From examining the clever lyrics and surprising rhymes, one can (4) _____ that rappers spend lots of time and effort on their craft. One day perhaps rap's foes will (5) _____ that they have been unfair in their criticism of this art form.

(Answers are on page 148.)

Meet Words 161 to 165!

161. Benevolent comes from the Latin word *benevolens*; *bene* means "well" and *volens* means "to wish." Therefore, this adjective describes a person or act that is *kindly* or *well-meaning*. Charitable organizations may be annoying, but they mean to do well and are clearly benevolent.

162. To resume is to *continue*. After a telephone interruption, the narrator must resume preparing dinner.

163. Brashly is the adverb form of brash. A person who is brash is a little more than confident. Such a person might act too quickly and, in doing so, appear rude.

164. Dwindle means to *decrease* in size or amount. You would not want your savings account to dwindle, would you?

165. A miser is someone who doesn't like to part with his money. (Maybe he hides it under the mattress so no one can get it!) The narrator really shouldn't feel like a miser, since he actually makes an annual donation of $50.

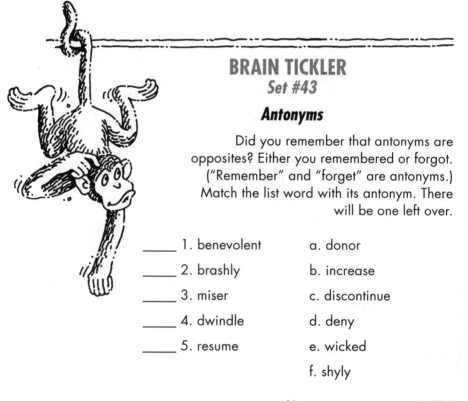

BRAIN TICKLER
Set #43

Antonyms

Did you remember that antonyms are opposites? Either you remembered or forgot. ("Remember" and "forget" are antonyms.) Match the list word with its antonym. There will be one left over.

_____ 1. benevolent   a. donor

_____ 2. brashly   b. increase

_____ 3. miser   c. discontinue

_____ 4. dwindle   d. deny

_____ 5. resume   e. wicked

                          f. shyly

(Answers are on page 148.)

THE VERBAL ANALOGY BRIDGE

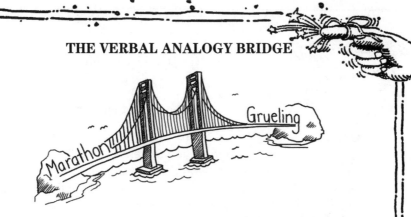

In Chapter 4, you learned about verbal analogies. In this chapter you will learn about the importance of using a "bridge" in solving verbal analogies.

Here is how the bridge works. You know that a verbal analogy consists of two pairs of words. What you want to do is create a sentence that clearly describes the relationship between the given pair. Consider the following problem:

marathon : grueling :: _____ : benevolent

Examining the given pair, you might produce a bridge that reads like this: "A marathon is an example of something that is grueling." Having done so, you would look to find a word that creates the same relationship in the second pair. In this case, you'd be looking for an example of something that would be "benevolent." ("Charity" would do the trick.)

For each of these analogies, supply the correct answer and the bridge you created.

1. collector : memorabilia :: miser : _____
   a. misery   b. confusion   c. objects   d. money
   Your bridge: _____

2. monotonous : varied :: dwindle : _____
   a. fade   b. contribute   c. increase   d. introduce
   Your bridge: _____

(Answers are on page 148.)

BRAIN TICKLER
Set #44

Words in Context

Choose the correct form of the list word to complete the sentence. Look for context clues. The list words are: grueling, serenity, multitude, solicitors, resolve, assure, monotonous, pursuit, conclude, infer, benevolent, resume, brashly, dwindle, and miser.

1. Running a marathon in this kind of hot, sticky weather just has to be a(n) _____ experience.

2. The rookie _____ predicted that he would lead his team in scoring, rebounding, and assists.

3. The salesman _____ the customer that the appliance would last for at least ten years.

4. After his sophomore year, James decided to travel, after which he hoped to _____ his college studies.

5. Have you ever called someone and been placed on hold? And were you forced to listen to that _____ recording of canned music and boring ads?

6. Sarah is a very kind woman; her work with disabled veterans is just one example of her _____ deeds.

7. The emcee said, "Before we _____ today's ceremony, let me thank you all for attending. I hope to see you again next year."

8. From your negative comments, I can _____ that you really don't like your math teacher.

9. Some _____ seek contributions to charitable causes, but many are more concerned with selling a product or service.

10. If Jerry weren't such a(n) _____, he'd probably be willing to spend some money on some new clothes.

11. Acadmic excellence is not the result of either good instruction or hard work or intelligence, but a _____ of factors.

12. I happen to enjoy several recreational _____, including biking, running, and fishing.

13. After a hectic day in the city, Henry enjoys the _____ of a walk along the seashore.

14. Because of a series of injuries and bad trades, the team's victory total _____ from one year to the next.

15. Terry _____ to begin a program of diet and exercise in order to lose some of the weight he had recently gained.

(Answers are on page 148.)

ON YOUR OWN

Imagine a conversation that you might have with a solicitor who is determined to sell you a product or service that you do not need. Use at least five of the list words in your conversation.

Solicitor: _____

_____

You: _____

_____

Solicitor: _____

_____

You: _____

_____

Solicitor: _____

_____

You: _____

_____

THE LAST WORD

The English language has lots of words that refer to character, or personality. If we say that a man acts brashly, we acknowledge his confidence, yet we also suggest that he might have a bit too much of it. Thus, we can infer that "brashly" has a somewhat negative connotation, or tone. What other list words refer to a person's character? Do they offer a positive, negative, or neutral connotation?

BRAIN TICKLERS—THE ANSWERS

Set #41, page 141

1. e
2. a
3. c
4. d
5. f

Set #42, page 143

1. monotonous
2. assure
3. pursuits
4. infer
5. conclude

Set #43, page 144

1. e
2. f
3. a
4. b
5. c

The Verbal Analogy Bridge, page 145

1. d (A collector is a person who likes to keep memorabilia.)
2. c ("Monotonous" is the opposite of "varied.")

Set #44, page 146

1. grueling
2. brashly
3. assured
4. resume
5. monotonous
6. benevolent
7. conclude
8. infer
9. solicitors
10. miser
11. multitude
12. pursuits
13. serenity
14. dwindled
15. resolved

CHAPTER TWELVE

Ozzie's Nine Lives
Using an Electronic Thesaurus

It's a cliché that cats have nine lives, but Ozzie, it seems, really does.

When Ozzie's predecessor, Poochie, was hit by a car, we promised my son that he could pick out another cat. At the North Shore Animal League, Ozzie was hard to miss. The size of one's fist, he was mostly black, with an irresistible white smudge right on his mouth.

Because he liked to play ball (a fairly unusual activity for a cat) and because he seemed so agile, my son named him Ozzie, in honor of Ozzie Smith, the St. Louis Cardinals' shortstop whose defensive wizardry earned him the nickname "The Wizard of Oz."

Before long we could tell that something wasn't right. Ozzie would huddle by the refrigerator's exhaust, one of the warmer spots of the kitchen, and he gradually became less and less vigorous. The veterinarian disclosed that Ozzie was suffering from such a nasty case of ear mites. An infection had ensued, and surgery would be necessary. It would be the first of many trying episodes.

Several years later, when Ozzie was an adult (remember that one cat year equals about seven human years), we were enjoying a fairly large dinner party. For an early spring night, the weather was unusually warm, so I opened the living room window. Later that evening, when our guests had left and we had begun to clean up, Ozzie was nowhere to be found. Apparently, he had escaped through the open window. We could not find him that night. Distraught as we were, we slept poorly.

The next day we embarked upon a plan to find him. First, we scoured our neighborhood, but to no avail. Then we posted "Lost Cat" signs on every block. Over the next few days, as the phone would ring, we responded to one false sighting after another. Then the phone stopped ringing. We tried to resist morbid thoughts, but we could not keep them from our minds.

It was a gray day in mid-April. The chill had returned. Deciding to get on with our lives as well as we might in the post-Ozzie era, we returned to some degree of normalcy. To get some errands done, we piled into the car, and as I pulled out of the driveway, my wife called, "Stop! Stop! It's Ozzie!" There he was, resting in the dirt, trying to absorb the day's few warming rays of sunshine. Where he had gone for the better part of a week we would never know. Clearly, Ozzie wasn't talking.

A few years later Ozzie became seriously ill. It was evident that his joints had swelled and had begun to ache badly. It was hard for him to move. His actual illness was hard to diagnose, but it was clear that his immune system wasn't working properly. In effect, his body's defenses were attacking his own joints. Eventually his doctor found medication that worked, and his conditioned improved, but Ozzie would suffer several recurrences of this disease.

With a cat like this, it's hard to keep score of exactly how many lives he's already used up—and how many remain (at least, according to the cliché). As we like to say, it's a good thing he's cute.

Meet Words 166 to 170!

166. A cliché is an expression that has been overused. "It hit me like a ton of bricks" is an example of such an overused expression.

167. The predecessor is the one who comes before. For example, Ronald Reagan's predecessor in the White House was Jimmy Carter.

168. An agile person is one who can move swiftly and nimbly. Chris Paul's agility enables him to maneuver through and around vastly larger opponents.

169. Wizardry, though often performed by wizards, actually refers to *magic* of other kinds as well. The chef at Mama Lucia's displays his wizardry whenever he prepares his delicious shrimp parmigiana.

170. When an older politician runs for office, it's important to show that he's still a *vigorous* man. Voters prefer elected officials who are *energetic* and *dynamic*.

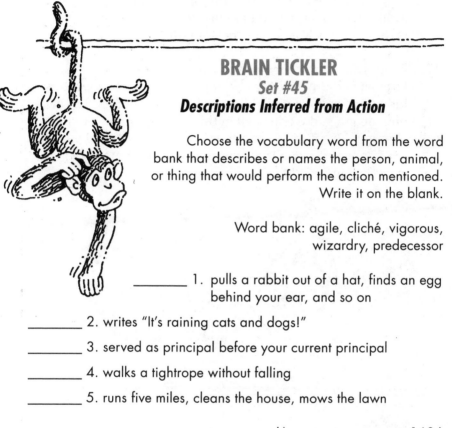

BRAIN TICKLER
Set #45
Descriptions Inferred from Action

Choose the vocabulary word from the word bank that describes or names the person, animal, or thing that would perform the action mentioned. Write it on the blank.

Word bank: agile, cliché, vigorous, wizardry, predecessor

_____ 1. pulls a rabbit out of a hat, finds an egg behind your ear, and so on

_____ 2. writes "It's raining cats and dogs!"

_____ 3. served as principal before your current principal

_____ 4. walks a tightrope without falling

_____ 5. runs five miles, cleans the house, mows the lawn

(Answers are on page 160.)

Meet Words 171 to 175!

171. To *disclose* means to *reveal*. After the veterinarian looked Ozzie over, he was able to disclose, or reveal, that Ozzie was suffering from ear mites.

172. To *ensue* means to *follow*. (It comes from the Latin *insequi*, which means "to come afterward.") After Ozzie's very serious ear mites infection, surgery necessarily ensued.

173. Anyone who has lost a pet would feel distraught, or *upset*. We grow very attached to our pets, and this kind of distress is understandable.

174. Embark has two meanings. Its original meaning is to board a ship, but its more common meaning, arising from the first, is to *begin* any kind of journey or enterprise.

175. Scour also has two meanings. The first, reserved for the kitchen and other dirt-prone spots, refers to the vigorous kind of cleaning a really dirty frying pan requires. The second meaning, the one used in this passage, means to pass over quickly, often in search of something. When the narrator discovered that Ozzie was missing, he scoured the streets of his neighborhood.

BRAIN TICKLER
Set #46

Words in Context

Use one of these list words (embark, scour, disclose, ensue, distraught) to complete the following sentences.

1. A child who has done something naughty may worry about the punishment that will _____.

2. The police officers will _____ the area, hoping to find a witness or a weapon.

3. Do you know what time your ship will _____?

4. I had hoped that consulting an encyclopedia would _____ the necessary information, but I now saw that I would have to research the topic further.

5. For a while you will understandably feel _____, but eventually you will get over this loss.

(Answers are on page 160.)

Meet Words 176 to 180!

176. Avail is a word that is commonly used as a verb and a noun. As a verb, it means to be of good use. If you are building a deck, you'll need to avail yourself of a saw and a drill. As a noun, it means *use* or *advantage*. The expression "to no avail" suggests an unsuccessful attempt.

177. Morbid thoughts are *gloomy* ones. It can be hard to be upbeat when you have good reason to worry about another's well-being.

178. If you're not feeling well, you might be able to diagnose your own illness, but you're more likely to ask a doctor to *recognize* and *identify* the problem.

179. When we are immune from something unpleasant (taxes, criminal charges, illness), we are *protected* from it. If a person's immune system breaks down (which is what happens to AIDS victims), all sorts of diseases could harm her.

180. To recur means to happen again. Therefore, a recurrence refers to a *reappearance* of a particular event. If you've ever been embarrassed in front of a large group, you'd probably do anything to avoid a recurrence.

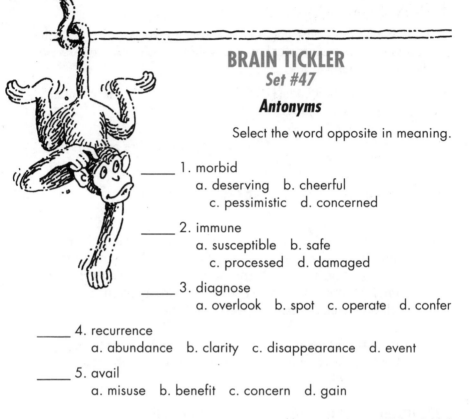

BRAIN TICKLER
Set #47

Antonyms

Select the word opposite in meaning.

_____ 1. morbid
    a. deserving   b. cheerful
      c. pessimistic   d. concerned

_____ 2. immune
    a. susceptible   b. safe
      c. processed   d. damaged

_____ 3. diagnose
    a. overlook   b. spot   c. operate   d. confer

_____ 4. recurrence
    a. abundance   b. clarity   c. disappearance   d. event

_____ 5. avail
    a. misuse   b. benefit   c. concern   d. gain

(Answers are on page 160.)

USING AN
ELECTRONIC THESAURUS

In Chapter 9, you learned how to use a standard thesaurus. If you've since managed to try out those skills, you've probably learned that one kind of thesaurus—the dictionary kind—is a lot easier and faster to use than the other kind. (That said, the indexed kind of thesaurus can't be beat for completeness of information.)

Well, there's another kind of thesaurus that's even easier to use. It may be the one you're most likely to use—the electronic thesaurus.

There are two kinds: the thesaurus that you'd find on its own Web site (similar to the online dictionaries described in Chapter 8) or those that you'd find in just about any word processing program.

Using an online thesaurus couldn't be easier. First, select one you'd like to use by typing "online thesaurus" into your browser. (If you've already selected an online dictionary and labeled it a "favorite," you're probably ahead of the game.) Next, simply type in the word under consideration and check out the results. For example, if you enter "agile" on the Merriam-Webster online thesaurus, you'll be given one result: you will be told to "see 'graceful.'" However, when you click on "graceful," you'll be directed to a large page that includes synonyms, antonyms, and other related words.

Nowadays you'd have a hard time finding a good word processing program that doesn't have a built-in thesaurus. And they're really easy to use.

All you have to do is place your cursor on a particular word (some programs ask you to highlight the word) and access the thesaurus. You might have to click on the word "Tools" on the tool bar and then find the thesaurus. There's always a shortcut for this kind of operation, and it won't be long before you find it and use it regularly.

When you don't know the meaning of a word, you're likely to use a dictionary. If you're after synonyms or antonyms, a thesaurus will be more helpful. You're most likely to search for synonyms when you're writing, and that's a great idea. The more you write, the more you'll notice that you tend to use the same words again and again. Using a thesaurus can expand your vocabulary, and it can help you become a more interesting writer.

BRAIN TICKLER
Set #48

Words in Context

Choose the correct list word to complete the follow-ing sentences. Look for context clues. The list words are: cliché, predecessor, agile, wizardry, vigorous, disclose, ensue, distraught, embark, scour, avail, morbid, diagnose, immune, and recurrence.

1. Even though we may lead less physically _____ lives as we grow older, it is still important for us to keep in good shape.

2. The children could not wait for their mother to _____ the eagerly anticipated ending to their favorite bedtime story.

3. Mr. Piorkowski was a splendid English teacher; every day his teaching _____ would enthrall his students.

4. If you are going to break school rules, you must be aware of the consequences that will _____.

5. Dana was anxious about taking the new job because she had heard so much about the talents of her _____.

6. Your teachers tell you that using fresh, original language is prefer-able to relying upon some old, timeworn _____.

7. During your stay, try to _____ yourself of the hotel's excellent fitness center.

8. Daniel's teacher accused him of looking at his neighbor's paper; thereafter, he kept his eyes focused straight ahead in order to avoid a(n) _____ of that embarrassing incident.

9. Nancy's ankle just wasn't feeling right, so she went to see her doctor for a(n) _____ and treatment.

10. Sandra's _____ reaction to learning of her uncle's death was understandable; the two had always been very close.

11. A tightrope walker is sure to be a(n) _____ individual; otherwise, he's bound to spend too much time in the safety nets!

12. When Julia realized that she had lost her bracelet, she and her friends _____ the cafeteria in search of it.

13. Anthony wanted to become a physician, so he _____ upon a course of study that would lead to admission to medical school.

14. Taylor has said so many nasty things to me over the years that I am practically _____ to her insults. They just don't bother me anymore.

15. Most of my friends thought the movie was exciting, but others found it _____, with its focus on bloody, unpleasant events.

(Answers are on page 160.)

ON YOUR OWN

Ozzie was able to bounce back from one difficulty after another, but Ponce de Leon was even more fortunate. According to legend, de Leon discovered the fountain of youth, the secret to remaining young forever. Pretend you are Ponce. Write a letter to a close friend in which you boast of your discovery. Use at least five list words in your letter. Feel free to exaggerate!

THE LAST WORD

Not everyone can display wizardry when writing. However, if you embark upon a plan to do so, you will not be distraught by the ensuing results. Take a look at these five clichés. Try to understand what each one means. Then write the same idea in your own, original way. Have some fun with these.

1. He was quiet as a mouse.

2. Mind your own business.

3. The moment of truth arrived.

4. Tomorrow is another day.

5. That guy is as nutty as a fruitcake.

BRAIN TICKLERS—THE ANSWERS

Set #45, page 153

1. wizardry
2. cliché
3. predecessor
4. agile
5. vigorous

Set #46, page 154

1. ensue
2. scour
3. embark
4. disclose
5. distraught

Set #47, page 156

1. b
2. a

3. a
4. c
5. a

Set #48, page 158

1. vigorous
2. disclose
3. wizardry
4. ensue
5. predecessor
6. clichés
7. avail
8. recurrence
9. diagnosis
10. distraught
11. agile
12. scoured
13. embarked
14. immune
15. morbid

CHAPTER THIRTEEN

Enough to Eat
Importing New Words

Imagine this scene. It starts out familiar, but it soon turns scary.

One day you look in the mirror, and you think you've put on some weight. You perceive the need for a diet. You begin to cut your calories and lose some of that weight, but no matter how much you lose, you never feel thin enough. Your friends and family say that you are positively emaciated, but in your mind you're still frightfully obese. You continue to diet and lose weight, but always your body ideal seems elusive. No matter how much weight you lose, you just can't reach your goal. Before very long, your once innocent diet becomes a serious health risk.

You are suffering from anorexia nervosa.

No one really knows what causes anorexia nervosa, but theories certainly do abound. Some researchers think the problem begins with pressure in our society to be thin and attractive. (Anorexia afflicts females far more often than males.) There is plenty of evidence in the entertainment industry to support this claim. Others think that the cause can be found in families whose members become too dependent upon each other. The girls in these families hope to impede the normal growth process. They restrict their diets in order to remain children and thereby maintain the parent-child relationship that the family counts on. Some researchers believe that anorexia is an attempt to assert self-control in order to repel pressures from an overly close family.

Anorexia nervosa can be very hard to diagnose. This is because many victims diet furtively—they don't want people to know of their unusual eating habits—and also because they don't think that their decreasing body weight is a problem. Only when other medical problems surface does an anorexia sufferer receive medical attention. The medical problems can be harsh. This much weight loss can lead to depression and severe fatigue. Other manifestations of this disorder are low blood pressure, disturbances in the heart rate, abdominal pain, and anemia.

Of course, an anorexia sufferer must first gain some weight, but the treatment of anorexia must focus on more serious fundamental psychological issues. Some individuals experience only a single episode of anorexia, but others have to deal with a fluctuating pattern of weight gain and weight loss. In any case, a good treatment program will include counseling (family therapy might be appropriate), medical care, and nutrition education.

Meet Words 181 to 185!

181. To perceive is to *notice* or *recognize*. In a typical family sitcom, a wife will become annoyed if her husband fails to perceive that she has changed her hairstyle. The noun form of the word, perception, refers to the act of noticing.

182. Emaciated goes beyond thin. When you think of the bodies of starvation victims, you have a good sense of what it means to be emaciated.

183. Obese goes in the opposite direction. Health officials in this country are concerned that we are eating too much and exercising too little. The result? A nation with an obesity problem.

184. Elusive means *hard to find, hard to pin down*. Hockey great Wayne Gretzky was smaller, weaker, and slower than most players. In a physical sense alone, the source of his greatness was elusive.

185. To abound is to exist in abundance, *to be plentiful.* (In fact, the two words have the same root: from the Latin *abundare,* "to overflow.") Visitors to this country notice that, when it comes to shopping for clothing or food, choices abound.

TAKING NOTE OF PERCEIVE

The word "perceive" comes from the Latin *percipere*, which means "to take hold of" or "to comprehend." We perceive in two ways. We may become aware of something through the senses, or we may recognize or observe something intellectually. From the corner of your eye, you may perceive the flight of a blue jay in your back yard. As you lie in bed, wiping sleep from your eyes, you may perceive the gentle aroma of coffee brewing in the kitchen. Or you may perceive Shakespeare's point—and humor—when he writes, "My mistress' eyes are nothing like the sun."

BRAIN TICKLER
Set #49

Antonyms

Match the list word with the word most nearly opposite in meaning. There will be one left over.

_____ 1. perceive   a. skinny

_____ 2. emaciated   b. grouchy

_____ 3. obese   c. apparent

_____ 4. elusive   d. overlook

_____ 5. abound   e. lack

                     f. overfed

(Answers are on page 173.)

Meet Words 186 to 190!

186. To afflict is to visit some kind of trouble upon someone or something. For some reason, anorexia afflicts more females than males.

187. To impede is to halt progress. According to one theory, anorexia sufferers attempt to impede the normal process of their own physical development.

188. Anorexia victims go to great lengths to restrict, or *limit*, their caloric intake. They believe that they can reduce their weight by limiting the calories they consume.

189. If you wish to maintain a certain relationship, you hope to *keep* it as it is. In much the same way, maintenance workers keep a facility just as it is.

190. Assert comes from the Latin *asserere*, "to join" or "to claim." It means to state positively and with great confidence. A confident lawyer will assert his client's innocence.

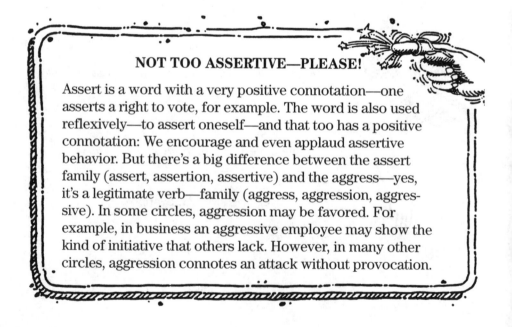

NOT TOO ASSERTIVE—PLEASE!

Assert is a word with a very positive connotation—one asserts a right to vote, for example. The word is also used reflexively—to assert oneself—and that too has a positive connotation: We encourage and even applaud assertive behavior. But there's a big difference between the assert family (assert, assertion, assertive) and the aggress—yes, it's a legitimate verb—family (aggress, aggression, aggressive). In some circles, aggression may be favored. For example, in business an aggressive employee may show the kind of initiative that others lack. However, in many other circles, aggression connotes an attack without provocation.

BRAIN TICKLER
Set #50

Now a Noun

Each of these five list words has a noun form:
afflict, impede, restrict, maintain, and assert.
Insert the correct noun form in the proper space.
(If you can do so, you will have learned ten
additional words!)

Anorexia nervosa is a very serious (1) _____
that affects more females than males. Some
researchers believe that a main cause of the illness is a person's
(2) _____ of his individuality and self-control; sometimes diet
offers the only way a person can show others that he or she is in
charge of that life. The illness's chief symptom, a substantial loss
of weight, results from a pattern of severe dietary (3) _____.
The resulting health problems pose a real (4) _____ to normal
activity and functioning: anorexia victims are often too frail and sickly
to conduct their lives as they usually do. Most experts agree that a
patient is not cured until he or she demonstrates (5) _____
of a proper body weight.

(Answers are on page 173.)

Meet Words 191 to 195!

191. To repel is to *turn or drive
back*. An army may repel its
opponent's advance. One of
the first things you learn
about magnetism is that
opposite poles attract and
the same poles repel.

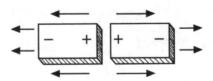

192. Furtively is the adverb form of furtive, which means secretive or sneaky. It's a good word to describe the eating habits of anorexics, who often don't want their loved ones to know how little they're actually consuming.

193. A manifestation is a *sign* or *expression*. It could also be a *symptom*, as it used in the anorexia passage. The word manifest (it comes from the Latin *manifestus*, which means "struck by the hand," or "near at hand," or "evident") can be used either as a verb (to make plain, or to show) or as an adjective (evident).

194. That which is fundamental is *basic* and *necessary*. There's no doubt that anorexics need to adjust their diets and their weight, but more fundamental to their well-being are the psychological issues that led to the problem in the first place.

195. Fluctuating, as used in the opening passage, is the adjective form of fluctuate, which means to move back and forth or up and down, as waves do. (That's not surprising, because the Latin word *fluctuare* means a "flowing wave.") Unfortunately, it also describes the weight gain-and-loss patterns of some anorexics who attempt to recover.

BRAIN TICKLER
Set #51

Nuts or Not?

Read each sentence to decide if the underlined vocabulary word is used correctly in context. If the meaning is ludicrous, write "Nuts" in the blank space. If the sentence makes sense, write "Not" in the blank space.

_____ 1. Jerry decided to wear his favorite Armani suit in an attempt to repel some of the women at the party.

_____ 2. Because she couldn't figure out the answer to #4, Samantha furtively stole a look at Amanda's paper.

_____ 3. A clear manifestation of superior writing is an author's ability to create a wonderful image.

_____ 4. Solving complex algebraic equations is a fundamental skill that very few kindergarten students manage to master.

_____ 5. Tammi's grades keep fluctuating: On one assignment she gets a 72, and then on the next she earns a 90.

(Answers are on page 173.)

THE IMPORT-EXPORT BUSINESS OF WORDS

As you certainly know, the United States exports many, many words all around the world. As a result, English words (or variations of them) become parts of many other languages. How does this happen? Through the two channels of commerce and culture! A number of years ago, you might have been surprised to travel to a foreign city and see a McDonald's restaurant, or a Starbuck's, or someone wearing American clothing brands or driving an American-made vehicle. You wouldn't be surprised nowadays, because these events are common.

Just as America exports products, this nation exports culture. You probably know that American television shows and films are broadcast around the world and that teenagers everywhere listen to American songs and CDs.

In the process, American words find their way into the vocabularies of other languages.

But you need to be aware that this import-export business is a two-way street. We Americans import words from other nations, cultures, and languages, too. This is especially evident when you consider the foods we enjoy. Do you like a hot, crispy croissant (France) to start the morning? How about a baguette (France) with some brie (France)? Maybe you're partial to bialys (Poland)? Do you like to stop at a café (France, Italy) for an espresso (Italy)? Or maybe you like a steaming cappuccino (Italy)?

When you decide to stop for lunch, you might opt for a slice of pizza (Italy). Then again, maybe you're more in the mood for a frankfurter (Germany). Or perhaps you'd like a pita (Greece) sandwich, stuffed with felafel (the Middle East).

Do you get the picture? Let's hope so, since we haven't even thought about dinner: spaghetti or goulash or sushi or chop suey or . . . .

BRAIN TICKLER
Set #52

Words in Context

Choose the correct form of the list word to complete the following sentences. Look for context clues. The list words are: perceive, emaciated, obese, elusive, abound, afflict, impede, restrict, maintain, assert, repel, furtively, manifestation, fundamental, and fluctuating.

1. The students protested in an attempt to
_____ their displeasure with the school's new dress policy.

2. Because of the _____ weather conditions in England, residents of that nation may not know exactly what to wear: one minute it's sunny, and the next it's raining.

3. In today's National Basketball Association, talented players _____; however, not every talented player is a good citizen on and off the court.

4. Reading and writing are _____; they are the foundation upon which all other learning builds.

5. Not everyone can _____ a difference between brands of cola, but the manufacturers would like consumers to believe there's a huge difference.

6. James permitted his eyes to glance _____ at his neighbor's exam.

7. Elected officials must _____ open communication with the citizens who voted them into office.

8. If you don't wish to become _____, you will need to develop healthy habits involving food and exercise.

9. Often the very first _____ of a leaky pipe is some slight discoloration in the walls and ceilings.

10. The accident blocked one lane of traffic and also served to _____ our progress, which is why we're twenty minutes late.

11. Despite all the money that's gone into research, cancer still _____ a sizable portion of the population.

12. The primary purpose of those huge cement flowerpots is not to create an attractive environment, but to _____ any driver and vehicle determined to damage the building.

13. A cure for cancer has been _____, despite the fact that researchers have been trying for half a century to find one.

14. Some of these new outfits seem to have been designed for _____ women, since they look silly on women with normal figures.

15. If you are interested in improving your grades, you will need to study harder and _____ your video game and television time.

(Answers are on page 173.)

ON YOUR OWN

We keep drawing your attention to the fact that the same word will appear in different forms, or as different parts of speech. In fact, the word "draw" can be a verb (to draw), a noun (drawing), or an adjective (drawn). Your task here is to create a sentence that uses the list word in a new form. The first is done for you.

1. perceive → noun

   His delayed perception of the other vehicle resulted in the accident.

2. obese → noun

3. elusive → verb

4. abound → adjective

5. afflict → noun

6. impede → noun

7. assert → adjective

8. manifestation → verb

9. furtively → verb

10. fluctuating → verb

THE LAST WORD

Are you familiar with the expression "manifest destiny"? You have probably come across it in your study of American history. Basically, this principle said it was the destiny (or fate) of the United States to dominate the Western Hemisphere, and that the nation could manifest (or show) that destiny by expanding from the Atlantic Ocean all the way to the Pacific. Not so fast, some might assert. After all, what happens when one people's destiny clashes with the destiny of other peoples (in this case, the many tribes of Native Americans already living in that path)? Well, then manifest destiny can be viewed as a thinly veiled excuse for colonialism. Thus, vocabulary and history intersect!

BRAIN TICKLERS—THE ANSWERS

Set #49, page 165

1. d
2. f
3. a
4. c
5. e

Set #50, page 167

1. affliction
2. assertion
3. restriction
4. impediment
5. maintenance

Set #51, page 168

1. nuts
2. not
3. not
4. nuts
5. not

Set #52, page 170

1. assert
2. fluctuating
3. abound
4. fundamental
5. perceive
6. furtively
7. maintain
8. obese
9. manifestation
10. impede
11. afflicts
12. repel
13. elusive
14. emaciated
15. restrict

CHAPTER FOURTEEN

All Pumped Up–
Home Runs and Steroids

A Brief History of Dictionaries

"There's a huge drive to deep right," the announcer cries, his voice shrill with excitement. "It's high, it's far, it's a home run!" As the brawny batter triumphantly circles the bases, the crowd cheers politely. However, their suspicion is nearly as audible as their pleasure. Where did those muscles come from? Was the home run legitimate? Should it count in this particular game? Should it count as fans consider a player's career? And what about the sport's records?

The fans have every right to their cynicism. Due to the widespread use in sports of anabolic steroids, the lords of baseball (and other sports, professional and amateur) must accept that the very integrity of the game is at stake.

Anabolic steroids are a group of naturally occurring and synthetic chemicals. Derived from the male hormone testosterone, these steroids were developed originally to help cancer patients. Anabolic steroids promote weight gain and increase muscle mass. However, in recent years athletes have taken them hoping to improve their performance on the playing field. The problem with this is two-fold. First, steroid use gives one group of athletes an unfair advantage over those who refrain from using the drugs. Second, steroid users incur a great risk of psychological and physical side effects. These include unusually aggressive behavior, liver damage, strokes, and even cancer. (Recently, former baseball star Ken Caminitti, an acknowledged steroid user, died at the age of forty-one.) In 1974, the International Olympic Committee banned steroid use, but other sports have been much slower in realizing the drug's perils and in taking appropriate action.

Many old-timers openly express their displeasure with this epidemic abuse. They feel that performances enhanced by drugs are fraudulent. In 2004 President George W. Bush encouraged athletes and team owners to create a set of rules that will keep steroids out of sports.

However, many younger people are not as upset. A recent *New York Times* poll said that forty-one percent of people under the age of thirty are "not bothered by the idea that pro athletes use steroids." There are two possible reasons for this. One is that younger fans tend to see sports more as entertainment. They view huge baseball stars clubbing huge home runs as just a step up from professional wrestling. A second reason is that younger fans have grown up with knowledge of all kinds of enhancements. Whether surgical or chemical, whether intended for beauty or health, enhancements—anabolic steroids included—don't seem so out-of-the-ordinary to younger fans.

There's some evidence that very young student-athletes have begun to use steroids. Because they are so easily available on the Internet, because of pressure to excel from coaches and parents (yes, parents!), because some kids want to "get big," and because improved performance could bring a fat scholarship offer, some youngsters are stepping into some very dangerous territory.

Meet Words 196 to 200!

196. Shrill does not have a positive connotation. It means *high-pitched* to the point of unpleasantness. It might be the way a parent or teacher sounds when the well of patience has run absolutely dry.

197. We think of brawny defensive linemen in football or brawny heavyweight wrestlers or brawny construction workers. Brawny means *strong* or *muscular.*

198. That which is audible can be heard, but a tiny whisper may be inaudible. The root of the word comes from the Latin word *audire,* "to hear," and is present in related words such as audience and audio.

199. Legitimate has the same root as does *legal,* which is what the word means. A lawyer can help a business official

determine whether a particular transaction is legitimate or illegitimate. Bear in mind, too, that legitimate can also be a verb (its last syllable rhymes with "fate"), meaning *to justify*; just as often, we use the verb legitimize.

200. Cynicism is an interesting word, one whose meaning has changed. Originally a Cynic was one of an ancient Greek group of philosophers who believed that virtue was the only good. They became critical of the rest of society and its interests in material possessions and pleasures. (The Greek word *kynikos* means dog-like.) Now, in everyday use, the word is used to describe a certain state of mind, that of a person who tends to question other's motives.

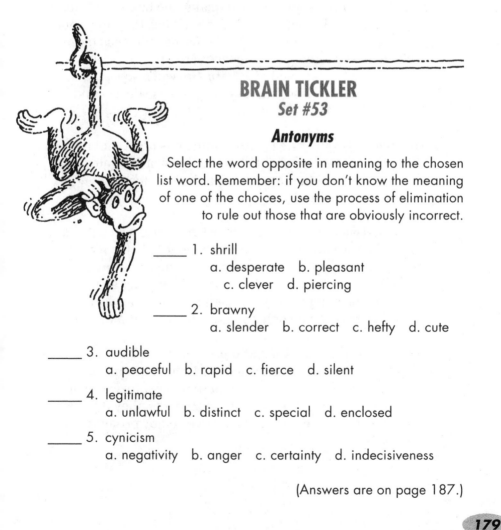

BRAIN TICKLER
Set #53

Antonyms

Select the word opposite in meaning to the chosen list word. Remember: if you don't know the meaning of one of the choices, use the process of elimination to rule out those that are obviously incorrect.

_____ 1. shrill
   a. desperate   b. pleasant
      c. clever   d. piercing

_____ 2. brawny
      a. slender   b. correct   c. hefty   d. cute

_____ 3. audible
   a. peaceful   b. rapid   c. fierce   d. silent

_____ 4. legitimate
   a. unlawful   b. distinct   c. special   d. enclosed

_____ 5. cynicism
   a. negativity   b. anger   c. certainty   d. indecisiveness

(Answers are on page 187.)

Meet Words 201 to 205!

201. An amateur is in one sense a person, often an athlete, who does not get paid for his or her performance. But the word can also have a strongly negative connotation, meaning someone whose efforts are so poor he does not deserve any pay! So, whether you're hiring a plumber or attending a sporting event, you might prefer to spend your money on a professional. (The word can also serve as an adjective.)

202. Integrity is another word with several meanings. One suggests the state of being whole or unbroken; for example, we might say that, despite the earthquake, the building's sound construction maintained its integrity. (It has the same root as integer—a whole number.) Another meaning has more to do with one's morality. This meaning refers to qualities we admire, like *honesty* and *sincerity*. So, when we say that steroids threaten baseball's integrity, we use the second meaning.

203. That which is synthetic is *man-made*; it is not found in nature. However, we might also use this word to refer to a gesture or an action that appears to be *insincere*. (Synthetic, often in plural form, can also appear as a noun.)

204. Derive derives from the Latin word *derivare*, which literally means "to turn a stream from its channel." That is why the word means *to get* or *receive* from a particular source. Steroids derive from male hormones. In another sense, it is similar in meaning to "*infer*": Even knowing the word's origin, we may not be able to derive its present meaning.

205. Promote comes from the Latin *promovere* (*pro* means forward, and *movere* means move). Hence, when we promote a suggestion, we attempt to move it forward, or *advance* it. When schools promote students, they do the same. For the same reason, employees enjoy promotions.

BRAIN TICKLER
Set #54

Words in Context

Complete this paragraph using list words 201 to 205 (amateur, integrity, synthetic, derived, promote).

LeBron James is one of the most exciting athletes to enter the National Basketball Association in many years. James decided to skip college and a(n) (1) _____ career, jumping straight to the professional level. It may be impossible to say exactly where James (2) _____ his remarkable physical gifts, but one thing is for sure: They are not the result of his using (3) _____ substances. No! James's talent may reflect the good luck of good genes, but his athletic excellence is the product of hard work and unrestrained joy in the game. That's why the league is hoping to (4) _____ James as its new symbol. League officials know that James's performance, personality, and work ethic can only help the league's (5) _____.

(Answers are on page 187.)

Meet Words 206 to 210!

206. Everyone knows it's a good idea to refrain from smoking cigarettes. Any time you can *avoid* doing something that is so potentially harmful to your body, you've done yourself a favor. Refrain can also be a noun (although that is not how it is used in the passage). It refers to the part of a song or a poem that is repeated at intervals, or to any catchy phrase.

207. Incur comes from the Latin *incurrere*, which means "to run toward." That explains why its current meaning is to bring upon oneself. If you elect to use steroids, you incur a great risk of unpleasant psychological and physical consequences.

208. Some people might not be aware of the perils—or *dangers*—of steroid use, but they should be, since it's all over the news these days. The verb form of the word, imperil, means to incur danger. Steroid users definitely imperil their health.

209. What's the appeal of steroids? When star athletes are aware of the perils of steroid use, why would they incur those kinds of risks? The answer is simple. Steroids not only enhance body size and strength; they also enhance performance on the playing field. (Enhance means *to improve* or *to increase*.) Let's not lose sight of the bottom line: Enhanced performance means an enhanced contract!

210. Fraudulent is the adjective form of fraud. A person who commits a fraudulent act hopes to deceive others. Therefore, fraudulent means *phony* or *fake*. And that's why sports fans simply don't know whether they can put their trust in today's athletes and the performances they produce.

BRAIN TICKLER
Set #55

Descriptions Inferred from Comments

Choose the vocabulary word from these list words (refrain, incur, peril, enhance, fraudulent) that describes the person who is making the comment.

_____ 1. "I have always wanted to strap a parachute on my back and jump out of an airplane. Now there's a thrill!"

_____ 2. "After smoking cigarettes for twelve years, I have finally decided to give it up."

_____ 3. "The best part about lifting weights is that I can actually see myself get bigger and stronger."

_____ 4. "I know that I'm really not a generous person, but I want people to think I am."

_____ 5. "I know what eating properly will do for my overall health, and I am determined to purchase and consume the proper foods and thereby bring about the desired result."

(Answers are on page 187.)

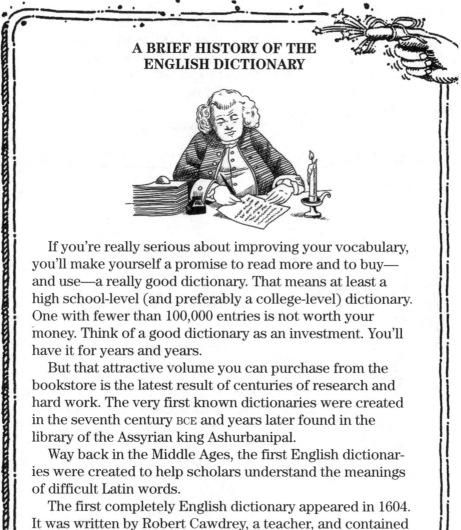

A BRIEF HISTORY OF THE ENGLISH DICTIONARY

If you're really serious about improving your vocabulary, you'll make yourself a promise to read more and to buy— and use—a really good dictionary. That means at least a high school-level (and preferably a college-level) dictionary. One with fewer than 100,000 entries is not worth your money. Think of a good dictionary as an investment. You'll have it for years and years.

But that attractive volume you can purchase from the bookstore is the latest result of centuries of research and hard work. The very first known dictionaries were created in the seventh century BCE and years later found in the library of the Assyrian king Ashurbanipal.

Way back in the Middle Ages, the first English dictionaries were created to help scholars understand the meanings of difficult Latin words.

The first completely English dictionary appeared in 1604. It was written by Robert Cawdrey, a teacher, and contained just over 3,000 words. This first dictionary specialized in difficult words. Therefore, it was called *The Table Aphabetical of Hard Words.* Over 100 years later, Nathan Bailey compiled a dictionary of about 60,000 words. It included hard words, as well as general English words.

The year 1755 was an important one for dictionaries because in that year Samuel Johnson published his *A Dictionary of the English Language.* In order to give examples of words in use, Johnson included quotes from many of the best English writers.

In the early 1800s, Noah Webster created a dictionary for American English. It contained over 70,000 entries. Ever since, the name "Webster" has become nearly synonymous with American English dictionaries. In fact, *Webster's Third New International Dictionary* is probably the most comprehensive dictionary of American English. It contains nearly 500,000 entries.

BRAIN TICKLER
Set #56

Words in Context

Choose the correct list word to complete the following sentences. Remember that the form of the word may differ slightly. Look for context clues. The list words are: shrill, brawny, audible, legitimate, cynicism, amateur, integrity, synthetic, derive, promote, refrain, incur, perils, enhance, and fraudulent.

1. Dentists assure their patients that regular brushing and flossing will _____ good dental health.

2. During the lecture only two sounds were _____: the professor's excited voice and the students' pencils, rapidly scratching notes onto paper.

3. When James brought home his disappointing report card, he anticipated—and heard—his mother's _____ reaction.

4. If you don't pay your taxes on time, you may _____ an additional penalty.

5. Sam _____ his annoying sense of humor from his father's side of the family, a large group of jokesters and pranksters.

6. When he brought the football team to the weight room, Coach had a saying he was fond of repeating: "I like 'em _____, not scrawny!"

7. John was not thrilled with his first quarter grades, but he discovered thereafter that good study habits would _____ his academic results.

8. The college's best player faced a difficult decision: If he went pro, he would have to give up his _____ standing, not to mention his scholarship.

9. Rock climbing can be an exciting sport, but who can overlook its obvious _____?

10. The salesman admitted that natural fibers were cool and attractive, but he reminded his customer that _____ materials required less care.

11. "You have behaved selfishly before," Jim explained to his brother, "so you must understand why I greet this latest promise with _____."

12. When Mr. Simmons realized that Jack had a(n) _____ point about a particular test question, he agreed to change the boy's grade.

13. There are lots of problems with plagiarism, not least of which is the possibility that a teacher will discover that the work is _____.

14. The architect argued against a modern renovation; she said that returning the house to its original state would maintain the _____ of the original design.

15. It's best to _____ from smoking altogether; if you never start, you'll never have to worry about stopping.

(Answers are on page 187.)

ON YOUR OWN

Write a letter to the editor of your school newspaper. In this letter, either defend or criticize young people's attitude toward steroid use. Use at least five of this chapter's list words in your letter.

THE LAST WORD

A knowledge of prefixes can help a reader derive a word's meaning. Take a look at synthetic, for example. The prefix *syn* means "together," and the word as a whole means "put together" (as opposed to "occurring naturally"). The word "synchronize" works just about the same way: *syn* (together) plus *chronos* (time) leaves us with "at the same time." Some other familiar words fit this same pattern: synonym, synopsis, and syndicate.

BRAIN TICKLERS—THE ANSWERS

Set #53, page 179

1. b
2. a
3. d
4. a
5. c

Set #54, page 181

1. amateur
2. derived
3. synthetic
4. promote
5. integrity

Set #55, page 182

1. peril
2. refrain
3. enhance
4. fraudulent
5. incur

Set #56, page 184

1. promote
2. audible
3. shrill
4. incur
5. derived
6. brawny
7. enhance
8. amateur
9. perils
10. synthetic
11. cynicism
12. legitimate
13. fraudulent
14. integrity
15. refrain

CHAPTER FIFTEEN

King of the #7 Train
Words from Myths

The year was 1975, and Peter was approaching a crucial period in his life. He was turning twenty-one. For most young men on that particular threshold, what probably come to mind are graduation, employment, and all the rights and privileges of adulthood. But not for Peter. Peter was born with Down syndrome. For him, turning twenty-one meant that he could no longer attend school.

Though Peter would never accumulate more than a sight vocabulary (he would learn to recognize a small number of printed words), he was able to take care of his own bodily needs and he communicated effectively. He attended a small special education program in Queens, New York. Because of his amiable personality and the pride he took in his own work, Peter thrived there. But now he was too old to attend this program, and the city would no longer provide a free school bus to any of the area's other appropriate educational programs.

Some twenty-one-year-olds might be elated to know that their schooling was coming to a close. Peter, however, was a very proud young man, and a large part of his dignity was tied to the successes he had experienced in school. He did not look forward to hanging around the house with his parents, and his parents were not optimistic about that idea, either. Peter was a sociable guy—he needed to mingle with others—and he and his family feared too that his academic and social skills would deteriorate without the structure of a full day's activities.

There was only one solution to what seemed like a nasty predicament. As unlikely as it seemed, Peter would have to learn to travel on his own.

The area's best program was located in Corona, a neighborhood in Queens, which meant that Peter would need to take two buses and a subway. Then, at the end of the day, he'd have to reverse his commute. No wonder he was unsure at first, and his parents reluctant to let him attempt such a feat.

Before Peter could begin to attend the program, he would have to learn how to travel on his own. So the program sent a travel trainer, Mike, who would serve as Peter's mentor for at least a couple of months.

For two months, Peter learned to recognize the correct bus numbers, to pay the correct fare, change buses at the correct location (this was especially tricky), locate the #7 train, take it four stops to 103rd Street, and find his way from the station to his new school. And he learned these same steps in reverse.

He had to pay very close attention—things that other twenty-one-year-olds may take for granted required Peter's focus. He could not mumble to himself or engage in long, inappropriate conversations with strangers. He needed to get to school on time, and then he needed to find his way safely home. It was an intimidating task, but the day arrived when Peter could travel without Mike's help. He was then able to begin the next chapter of his life.

Meet Words 211 to 215!

211. A crucial moment is one upon which everything depends. Because Peter would no longer be able to attend his previous school, his twenty-first birthday became such a moment.

212. You may be familiar with the threshold of a doorway— usually a piece of wood or stone, situated right below the door. Just as that threshold marks the very beginning of the room, we use threshold also to name a *beginning* of some other undertaking.

213. A syndrome refers to a number of symptoms (or manifestations) that characterize a particular condition or disease. For example, Down syndrome is characterized by certain physical features and mild to severe learning problems.

214. To accumulate is to *gather* or build up. Because of his learning problems, Peter would never be able to accumulate a large reading vocabulary.

215. Most people would not mind being described as amiable: it means having a *friendly*, pleasing disposition. (You may come across the word "amicable," which comes from the same Latin origin and means the same thing.)

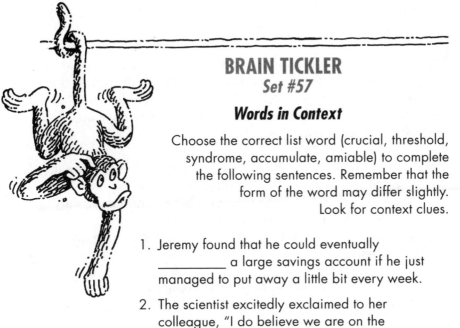

BRAIN TICKLER
Set #57

Words in Context

Choose the correct list word (crucial, threshold, syndrome, accumulate, amiable) to complete the following sentences. Remember that the form of the word may differ slightly. Look for context clues.

1. Jeremy found that he could eventually _____ a large savings account if he just managed to put away a little bit every week.

2. The scientist excitedly exclaimed to her colleague, "I do believe we are on the _____ of a great discovery!"

3. The teacher recognized all the signs of the "lousy test score" _____: long faces, pleas for a grade curve, and requests for extra credit.

4. The quarterback knew it was a(n) _____ moment in the game: if he failed to execute this play, his team would probably lose.

5. Because of his booming bass and his reputation as a demanding scholar, I was at first afraid of Professor Milhauser, but he turned out to be an easy-going, _____ fellow whom everybody liked.

(Answers are on page 200.)

Meet Words 216 to 220!

216. Peter thrived in school! He *succeeded* in school because much was asked of him and because he gave his all. Plants thrive, too, if they're treated properly, which shows that one can thrive physically, too.

217. You probably feel elated, or *thrilled*, when you earn a great grade on an important exam or when you score a goal that wins a game for your team. However, as Peter's case illustrates, what brings elation to one person can have little effect on another.

218. Dignity comes from the Latin word *dignitas*, which means "worth" or "merit." In the passage above, the word is used to refer to Peter's *self-respect*, but there's another equally common meaning. We need to treat others with dignity, with the kind of respect and *consideration* anyone deserves.

219. Do you look on the bright side? Do you see the glass as half full? If you do, then you are optimistic. Such a *hopeful* attitude may well endear you to others.

220. Mingle comes from the Middle English word *mengen*, which means "to mix." Sociable people like to mingle, but sometimes feelings do. Joy and sorrow might mingle at an event such as graduation, right?

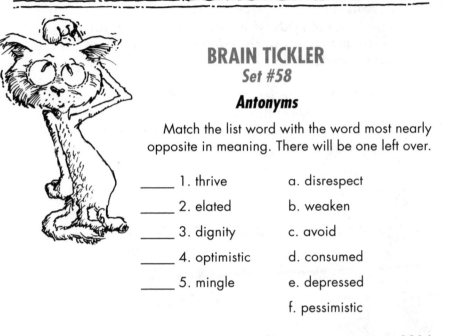

BRAIN TICKLER
Set #58

Antonyms

Match the list word with the word most nearly opposite in meaning. There will be one left over.

_____ 1. thrive   a. disrespect

_____ 2. elated   b. weaken

_____ 3. dignity   c. avoid

_____ 4. optimistic   d. consumed

_____ 5. mingle   e. depressed

                         f. pessimistic

(Answers are on page 200.)

Meet Words 221 to 225!

221. Peter had worked long and hard to improve his social skills, so the last thing he wanted was to see them deteriorate, or *worsen.*

222. A predicament is a *situation* in which you find yourself. Usually, it refers to a situation that is troubling in some way. It could be dangerous or embarrassing.

223. Reluctant comes from the Latin verb *reluctari*, which means "to resist." Peter's parents were reluctant, or *unwilling*, to let him embark upon his travel program, and it's not hard to understand their reluctance.

224. In Homer's great epic poem *The Odyssey*, a family friend by the name of—you guessed it—Mentor advises Odysseus's young son until Odysseus can return from his travels. Mentor now refers to any *adviser* or *guide*. The word can also be used as a verb.

225. For Peter, traveling all the way to his new school—and back again—was at first very intimidating, or *frightening*. (Of course, learning to use New York City's public transportation system might be intimidating to lots of people!)

BRAIN TICKLER
Set #59

Verbal Analogies

Complete each verbal analogy with one of these list words: deteriorate, predicament, reluctant, intimidating, mentor.

Remember how to read a verbal analogy.

Hot : cold :: rural : urban →
hot is to cold as rural is to urban

Remember to create a bridge for the given pair. Then use that same bridge to solve the analogy.

Try your best with these:

1. syndrome: symptoms :: scary : _____

2. improve : _____ :: amiable : grouchy

3. _____ : eager :: optimistic : unenthusiastic

4. accumulate : scatter :: _____ : pupil

5. _____ : impasse :: dignity : pride

(Answers are on page 200.)

WORDS FROM MYTHS

You've noticed that many of the words we've looked at have Latin origins. You may also have noticed that a few have Greek origins ("cynicism" is a recent example). What you might not be aware of is the number of English words that come from Greek and Roman stories, or myths.

This chapter contains one such word, "mentor," which comes from the name of a character in Homer's great epic *The Odyssey*.

Here's another word that you're probably familiar with: "marathon." Marathon was actually the name of a plain in Greece. In 490 BCE, Athenian troops there were about to be attacked by Persian invaders. Though badly outnumbered, the Athenians triumphed. The Athenians sent the great runner Phidippides to Athens with news of the Greek victory at Marathon. The distance between Marathon and Athens happens to be a little more than 26 miles, and it is this distance that constitutes a modern marathon.

However, the word "marathon" doesn't refer solely to a footrace. It has come to mean any event that takes a lot of time or covers a lot of distance or requires great endurance. You may have heard of dance marathons, popular a number of years ago. It has been said that the baseball season is a marathon, which explains why baseball enthusiasts should know better than to get too worked up over the outcome of a single game or two.

So you can see how the word's meaning has changed from a geographical location to a footrace to an endurance contest.

The appendix contains a list of other words that have their roots in Latin and Greek language and myths.

BRAIN TICKLER
Set #60

Words in Context

Choose the correct list word to complete the following sentences. Remember that the form of the word may differ slightly. Look for context clues. The list words are: crucial, threshold, syndrome, accumulate, amiable, thrive, elated, dignity, optimistic, mingle, deteriorate, predicament, reluctant, mentor, and intimidating.

1. A teacher needs to learn never to strip a child of his _____; when a child feels a teacher doesn't really respect him, he will soon lose respect for the teacher.

2. Jennie found herself in something of a(n) _____; she knew that if she befriended either Eleanor or Susie, she'd risk losing the friendship of the other.

3. On the night before he left for college, Jack could not sleep; he felt himself on the _____ of a life-altering experience.

4. My Aunt Esther has a(n) _____ personality; she gets along with absolutely everyone.

5. He had all the symptoms of the been-at-one-job-too-long _____: bored with the same old tasks, annoyed with his colleagues, and eager for his next day off.

6. Helen was just _____ when she learned she had won the lottery!

7. If you don't give it the proper care, you can be sure the condition of your vehicle will gradually _____.

8. It was a(n) _____ moment in the trial, and the defendant's fate hung in the balance.

9. Jonathan generally held a(n) _____ outlook, unlike his brother Phillip, who tended to dwell on the negative side of things.

10. Because of her hand injury, Stella was _____ to spike the volleyball and risk further damage to the hand.

11. When I began middle school, my older brother served as my _____, explaining to me how to deal with various academic and social situations.

12. Under the new coach, the team _____; the players reached their potential, and the team began to play as a unit.

13. Pat began collecting *Spiderman* and *Fantastic Four* in 1965, and within ten years he had _____ over 500 comic books.

14. Standing on the top of the slope and looking at its steep, winding turns, Willie was _____ enough to wonder why he had ever wanted to ski in the first place.

15. On the first day of school, most of the kids eagerly _____ with their old friends, but a few new students stood shyly on the sideline.

(Answers are on page 200.)

ON YOUR OWN

There's an art to creating a good teaching sentence. You want very much to make the meaning clear to your reader, so the sentence practically has to be redundant, which means that you might have to be a little repetitious. Consider this example from earlier in the chapter: "The scientist excitedly exclaimed to her colleague, 'I do believe we are on the _____ of a great discovery!'" The fact that a scientist is involved in making a great discovery, coupled with her excitement, led to the correct choice of "threshold."

Now it's your turn. Create five teaching sentences, using words introduced in this chapter.

THE LAST WORD

Reluctant is a handy word to know because it suggests an unwillingness to do something. When you're reading a book, you might be reluctant to look up the meaning of every word you didn't know, since such a practice would surely spoil the experience of a good read. But it's handy, too, for you to know a couple of other words that mean nearly the same thing. Take hesitant, for example, which suggests a degree of caution, but not as strong an unwillingness as reluctant. You might be hesitant about asking a tough teacher to adjust your grade on an essay. At the other extreme is loath (the adjective form of loathe, to hate), which suggests a very strong unwillingness. I would be loath to eat meat that was not sufficiently cooked.

BRAIN TICKLERS—THE ANSWERS

Set #57, page 193

1. accumulate
2. threshold
3. syndrome
4. crucial
5. amiable

Set #58, page 195

1. b
2. e
3. a
4. f
5. c

Set #59, page 196

1. intimidating
2. deteriorate
3. reluctant

4. mentor
5. predicament

Set #60, page 198

1. dignity
2. predicament
3. threshold
4. amiable
5. syndrome
6. elated
7. deteriorate
8. crucial
9. optimistic
10. reluctant
11. mentor
12. thrived
13. accumulated
14. intimidated
15. mingled

CHAPTER SIXTEEN

A Closer Look at the Patriot Act

Word Roots, Prefixes, and Suffixes

After the attacks on September 11, 2001, the nation felt an unfamiliar anxiety. Not since December 7, 1941, the day Japan attacked Pearl Harbor, did the citizens of this nation feel so vulnerable. What could America do to deter another attack? And, at the same time, how could we avoid jeopardizing those liberties we hold so dear? With September 11 serving as the catalyst, Congress passed the Patriot Act and President Bush signed it into law.

The Patriot Act undoubtedly has many advocates. They claim that the law has played a major role in foiling the deadly plans of those who would destroy America. These supporters argue that the Patriot Act gave law enforcement agencies the tools they needed to fight terrorism. Supporters argue that the Patriot Act included only incremental changes in existing laws, which had been used mostly to combat organized crime and drug trafficking. These laws needed to be updated anyway, in order to deal with new technologies and threats. Another benefit of the Act, they say, is that it facilitates information sharing among government agencies. Finally, the Act provides stiffer penalties against terrorists.

However, there's another side to the story. Critics of the Act complain that lawmakers, in their zeal to prevent another September 11, have overreacted in producing legislation that curtails civil liberties. Those who condemn the Act cite several key reasons. First, they say that the Act permits the government to imprison without trial non–United States citizens said to be threats to national security. Second, the Act does not require the government to provide legal counsel to those prisoners, nor does it require the government to make any announcement of the arrests. Third, critics claim that the Act expands the government's ability to issue wiretaps and to search people's homes without informing them.

After September 11, Americans knew that they could not maintain the status quo. An act of terrorism can destroy thousands or even millions of lives. Yet, in their determination to avoid another catastrophe, Americans cannot punish the innocent. Americans must learn from the mistakes of previous generations. One such mistake was the decision in 1941 to confine in camps thousands of innocent Americans of

Japanese descent. Not one of these persons was ever proven guilty of anti-American activity.

The best solution for now would be to keep informed. Read about this issue, and discuss it with friends. Thomas Jefferson believed that democracy would work only if involved citizens educated themselves properly.

Meet Words 226 to 230!

226. Anxiety is the unpleasant (for most people) state of *worry* or *concern*. After 9/11, many Americans had to adjust to an unpleasant sense of anxiety.

Major Mistake Territory!

The adjective form, anxious, actually has two meanings, which are related, but different enough to create confusion. The first means "uneasy": you may feel some anxiety when you're unsure of the answer to a tricky question your teacher asks you. The other meaning—and the one youngsters generally learn first—is "eager." Because Aunt Ginger's apple pie is legendary, I am anxious to get to dessert! (But I am not feeling anxious about eating it.)

227. Vulnerable comes from the Latin word *vulnerare*, "to wound." It means open to attack or criticism. So one can feel vulnerable physically, as well as emotionally. After the 9/11 attacks, Americans felt vulnerable. They had been wounded and might be wounded again.

228. To deter is to *discourage.*
We see all these shocking ads and data whose sole purpose is to deter us from smoking, yet somehow people continue to smoke cigarettes.

229. Have you seen the TV game show, *Jeopardy*? You probably have, but you may not know that to jeopardize is to place in harm's way. While we want to ensure our safety from terrorist attacks, we don't want to jeopardize, or *endanger*, the freedoms we wish to defend.

230. The word catalyst comes from the field of chemistry. It refers to a substance that speeds up a chemical reaction. But it has a more general meaning, too: it's the specific *cause* that gets something going. September 11 was the catalyst for the Patriot Act. Magic Johnson was the catalyst for those great Los Angeles Laker teams of the 1980s. He certainly got them going!

BRAIN TICKLER
Set #61

Descriptions Inferred from Action

Choose the vocabulary word (from anxiety, vulnerable, deter, jeopardize, and catalyst) that describes the person, animal, or thing that would do the action mentioned. Write that word in the blank.

Here's an example:

_____ You're riding in a very crowded elevator. You don't want to get sick, but five people are coughing, six are sneezing, and two are sniffling loudly.

What's the word? Vulnerable, of course!

Now try these:

1. _____ Stay home from work, do your work poorly, talk back to your boss, etc.

2. _____ You're watching the doctor lower a six-inch needle to your arm.

3. _____ An awful report card that convinces you to start taking school more seriously.

4. _____ The purpose of a TV ad aimed at those who would drive while intoxicated.

5. _____ You have three tests in school, you're playing for an athletic scholarship, your tooth hurts, and your wallet is empty.

(Answers are on page 214.)

Meet Words 231 to 235!

231. An advocate is a person who is in favor of something—and doesn't mind letting you know how she feels about that thing! Those in favor of the Patriot Act are its most outspoken advocates, or *supporters*. (Advocate can also be a verb: you can advocate for legislation to help the poor.)

232. You've probably heard of foil as a noun—as in the aluminum foil in which you wrap your sandwich. In this passage it's used as a verb, and it means to *frustrate* someone by preventing him from succeeding in his plans. In 2004, the Red Sox foiled the Yankees' attempt to get to the World Series.

233. An increment is an increase in size or amount, but quite often it refers to any of a number of small changes. When we speak of incremental changes in your vocabulary, we're referring to a gradual increase, as opposed to a sudden expansion of 1,000 words.

234. To facilitate is to make easy or possible. Some say the Patriot Act facilitates an easy exchange of important information among the governmental agencies that can make best use of it.

235. Zeal comes from the Greek word *zelos*. Both words refer to an eager interest in something. Usually this kind of devotion is seen as a positive trait, but you would not want to be considered overzealous (which can be very annoying) or a zealot (a person who is excessive in his devotion to a cause or principle).

BRAIN TICKLER
Set #62
Verbal Analogies

Complete each verbal analogy with one of these list words: advocate, foil, incremental, facilitate, zeal. A good strategy for dealing with analogies is to create a word bridge. For example, consider this analogy:

doctor : diagnose :: administrator : _____

What relationship exists between "doctor" and "diagnose"? You might conclude that one of a doctor's duties is to diagnose. Once you have that bridge, you would see that one of an administrator's duties is to facilitate.

1. anxiety : certainty :: criticize : _____

2. deter : hinder :: _____ : gradual

3. _____ : help :: jeopardize : endanger

4. vulnerable : invincible :: _____ : assist

5. professor : expertise :: fan : _____

(Answers are on page 214.)

Meet Words 236 to 240!

236. To curtail is to *limit* or *cut short*. Safety is a worthy goal, but do we want to curtail our civil liberties?

237. Condemn has a legal meaning and some general ones. The first, used less frequently, means to prove a person guilty: the jury condemned the defendant to life in prison. The second means to *disapprove* of strongly. A third is, in a way, a combination of two: to condemn a building means that it is unfit to live in.

238. Cite is another word with several meanings. As it is used in the passage above, it means to *quote* or *mention* as a way of proving. It can also mean to select someone as worthy of special honor, especially in the armed services. Finally, a court can cite a witness to appear in a trial.

Major Mistake Territory!

Cite is another of those homonym killers, fit company for *to-too-two* and *there-their-they're*. It might be confused with *site*, which means a particular place or location, such as a construction site. It might also be confused with *sight*, the sense of seeing.

239. With status quo, you get two new words for the price of one. Status means condition (the patient's status) or, in another sense, importance or reputation (a costly car is a status symbol). The status quo, however, is the state of things at a particular time. If you are interested in maintaining the status quo, you would not welcome any major changes.

240. Confine comes from the Latin word *confirmare*. *Con-* (or *com-*) means, in this case, "with," and *firmare* is a border. As a verb, the word means to keep within certain limits: all those innocent Japanese-Americans were confined in internment camps. Sometimes, you will hear it as a noun, usually in plural form, meaning "boundary." You might hear Red Sox fans refer to the cozy confines of Fenway Park.

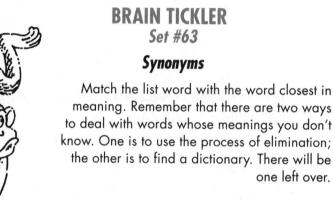

BRAIN TICKLER
Set #63

Synonyms

Match the list word with the word closest in meaning. Remember that there are two ways to deal with words whose meanings you don't know. One is to use the process of elimination; the other is to find a dictionary. There will be one left over.

_____ 1. curtail   a. mention

_____ 2. condemn   b. censure

_____ 3. cite   c. condition

_____ 4. status quo   d. imprison

_____ 5. confine   e. newcomer

                         f. curb

(Answers are on page 214.)

WORD ROOTS, PREFIXES, AND SUFFIXES

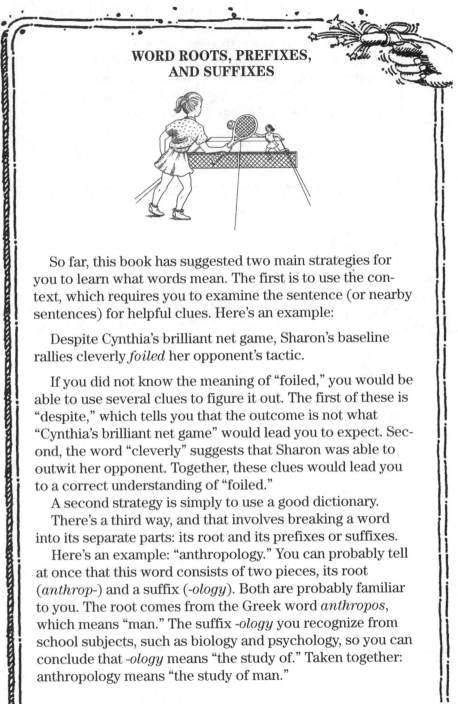

So far, this book has suggested two main strategies for you to learn what words mean. The first is to use the context, which requires you to examine the sentence (or nearby sentences) for helpful clues. Here's an example:

Despite Cynthia's brilliant net game, Sharon's baseline rallies cleverly *foiled* her opponent's tactic.

If you did not know the meaning of "foiled," you would be able to use several clues to figure it out. The first of these is "despite," which tells you that the outcome is not what "Cynthia's brilliant net game" would lead you to expect. Second, the word "cleverly" suggests that Sharon was able to outwit her opponent. Together, these clues would lead you to a correct understanding of "foiled."

A second strategy is simply to use a good dictionary.

There's a third way, and that involves breaking a word into its separate parts: its root and its prefixes or suffixes.

Here's an example: "anthropology." You can probably tell at once that this word consists of two pieces, its root (*anthrop-*) and a suffix (*-ology*). Both are probably familiar to you. The root comes from the Greek word *anthropos*, which means "man." The suffix *-ology* you recognize from school subjects, such as biology and psychology, so you can conclude that *-ology* means "the study of." Taken together: anthropology means "the study of man."

You can easily build upon what you know. Consider "phil-anthropy." *Phil-* comes from the Greek word *philos*, which means "loving." Therefore, philanthropy means "love of man," "charity," or "benevolence."

If you are studying a foreign language, you have already noticed that your knowledge of that language will further your understanding of word roots, prefixes, and suffixes.

You can donate a great deal of time and energy to the study of word roots, prefixes, and suffixes. In fact, you would have no trouble locating books that address this topic, and certainly your study of such a book would be worth your while.

What is more likely to happen is that, as your vocabulary expands, you will notice the kinds of patterns described above, and you will be able to use your knowledge of one word's parts to understand the meaning of another word.

Don't be hesitant to use the Internet. Simply use the key-words "word roots," and you will be provided with a range of helpful Web sites.

BRAIN TICKLER
Set #64

Words in Context

Choose the correct list word to complete the following sentences. Remember that the form of the word may differ slightly. Look for context clues. The list words are: anxiety, vulnerable, deter, jeopardize, catalyst, advocate, foil, incremental, facilitate, zeal, curtail, condemn, cite, status quo, and confine.

1. We've gotten some huge bills in recent weeks, so I'm afraid we will all have to _____ our spending for a little while.

2. Derek Jeter has served as the _____ for these Yankee teams; when he plays well, the whole team gets going.

3. Having a supportive family, a strong network of friends, and good study habits will _____ your adjustment to high school.

4. Some drivers are so lawless that even the presence of a patrol car at that intersection did not _____ them from making an illegal turn.

5. Phyllis experiences a great deal of _____ before a major test; her heartbeat quickens, her skin feels clammy, and she needs to calm herself down.

6. The Greek hero Achilles was _____ in only one area, his heel; otherwise, he could not be harmed.

7. The student liked to ramble when he answered a question, so the teacher asked her to _____ her remarks to the topic at hand.

8. In the Super Bowl, a great defense will usually _____ a superior offense, which is why defense almost always wins the big games.

9. At the start of the year, Mr. Graham so strongly _____ late-arriving students that eventually everyone began to get to class before the bell.

10. Jenny was less than thrilled with the _____ changes in her bonus; actually she had expected to receive much larger sums.

11. _____ for strict drug testing policies in professional sports easily outnumber critics of such policies.

12. My father, who much preferred maintaining the _____, was typically opposed to making major changes in his life.

13. Health professionals _____ cigarette smoking, insufficient exercise, and poor diet as the major problems affecting the younger generation.

14. "If you displayed the same _____ for cleaning your room as you display for playing video games," my mother said, "we would not be having this argument, and your room would be clean!"

15. Cyclists who refuse to wear helmets _____ their own safety and incur the risk of a serious head injury.

(Answers are on page 214.)

ON YOUR OWN

Here's the situation: Your school is about to apply a wide range of policies to improve school safety. These policies include the use of metal detectors, random searches of lockers and book bags, and the deployment of large numbers of security officials throughout the building. Write a letter to the school's principal, expressing either your approval or disapproval of the school's new policies. In your letter, be sure to use at least five of this chapter's list words.

THE LAST WORD

It's interesting how some words offer a sense of encouragement, while others have the opposite effect.

Take zeal, for example. There's a positive word, right? Everyone admires a healthy dose of enthusiasm. The same can be said for facilitate. We like people who can get things done, don't we? Along these same lines, there's advocate. What's wrong with someone speaking for a cause that he or she believes in?

Looking at just this chapter's list words, you should be able to find at least a half dozen that suggest discouragement. What are they?

BRAIN TICKLERS—THE ANSWERS

Set #61, page 205

1. jeopardize
2. vulnerable
3. catalyst
4. deter
5. anxiety

Set #62, page 207

1. advocate
2. incremental
3. facilitate
4. foil
5. zeal

Set #63, page 209

1. f
2. b
3. a
4. c
5. d

Set #64, page 211

1. curtail
2. catalyst
3. facilitate
4. deter
5. anxiety
6. vulnerable
7. confine
8. foil
9. condemned
10. incremental
11. advocates
12. status quo
13. cite
14. zeal
15. jeopardize

CHAPTER SEVENTEEN

The Hot Corner– Learning to Love Books

Word Games

When I was in middle school, I was not yet an avid reader. At the same time, I couldn't get enough of baseball.

In those days, without serious competition from football or basketball, baseball pretty much enjoyed a monopoly in terms of the interests of the American sports fan. I was no exception. My friends and I passed countless hours playing myriad variations of the game: softball, punchball, kickball, diamond ball, box baseball, flies up, stoopball, and, of course, the original. Given a round object and a pair of nimble hands, we managed to devise a set of rules that led to the completion of nine innings. Some of these rules were quite simple, others surprisingly intricate.

It may be a slight exaggeration to say that nothing that occupied the interlude between our games mattered quite as much as the games themselves. School, family, responsibilities, even social events managed to impart some occasional joy, yet they all somehow seemed prosaic compared to the excitement of the next baseball event.

One spring day I became ill, and this infirmity caused me to miss a day of school. I reached for a book I had taken from the school library. (I don't know if you can even imagine a life so arduous—a life without hundreds of cable channels or text messages or video games or the Internet—but somehow we managed.) The novel, entitled *The Hot Corner*, was about a teenage boy who wanted to play third base. He was physically talented, but he had been struck in the face by a hard line drive, and needed to overcome his fear of being struck again.

Now, looking back, I have to admit it doesn't seem like much of a premise for a novel, but I was thoroughly captivated. For a few hours, I forgot completely my painful sore throat. I wanted only to be brave enough to overcome adversity and excel on the playing fields. (The irony is that, as a lefty, I could never play third base, a position reserved only for right-handed throwers.) When I came to the end of the book, I was so sad that it was over, that I would have to return to my own life . . . until, perhaps, I could find another book just as wonderful.

And that is how one avid interest led to another. I read all the time these days, but I have to admit that I seldom find a novel as wonderful as *The Hot Corner*.

Meet Words 241 to 245!

241. Are you an avid reader? Or are you much less *enthusiastic* about books? Of course, sometimes an unenthused reader can become an avid one.

242. Have you ever played the board game Monopoly? The object of the game is to gain complete control of all the properties, and that's exactly what a monopoly is: that kind of complete control of something. Today, given the popularity of other sports, it may be hard to imagine a time when baseball monopolized (that's the verb form) the attention of America's sports fans.

243. In the passage above, myriad works as an adjective. It means *very many*. But you can also use it as a noun: today we can choose from a myriad of activities to pass the time.

244. You need nimble, or *quick*, *agile* hands to play baseball well. Do you know the nursery rhyme, "Jack be nimble, Jack be quick, Jack jump over the candlestick"?

245. An inventive child will devise many games to keep himself and his friends amused. A good science student will devise an experiment original enough to compete for first prize in the Science Fair. "Devise" means to *invent* or *develop*.

BRAIN TICKLER
Set #65

Descriptions Inferred from Comments

Choose the vocabulary word (avid, monopoly, myriad, nimble, devise) that describes the person making the comment or the thing that is being discussed. Write it on the blank.

_____ 1. "I own the only two drug stores in the neighborhood. I have absolutely no competition."

_____ 2. "Hmm . . . let me think of a way out of this fix."

_____ 3. "You think it's easy to juggle four balls at once? You think anyone can do it? Well, think again."

_____ 4. "Look at the size of this store! And look at the variety of merchandise! Why, there are watches, shoes, kitchenware, toiletries, toys, children's clothing. . . ."

_____ 5. "I'm crazy about that group. I'm a big fan. I've got all their CDs, and I hear there's a new one coming out next week. I can't wait to get my hands on it. I bet it's going to be great."

(Answers are on page 227.)

Meet Words 246 to 250!

246. That which is intricate can be hard to complete or follow or understand because of its complexity. This can be said of a tricky math problem, a line of poetry, a dance step, the machinery of a watch, or the set of rules to a game.

247. An interlude is anything that fills the time between two other events. The word comes from the Latin *interludium*; *inter-* means between, and *ludus* is a play. That's because originally an interlude was a short, humorous play performed between the acts of a longer, more serious one. Now its meaning has generalized to any event that fills a gap.

248. The time has come for this book to impart to you the meaning of "impart." Actually it has two meanings. One is to *deliver* (it is used this way in the passage above); the other is to *reveal*.

249. Do you know the difference between prose and poetry? Prose is regular writing, the kinds of sentences and paragraphs that form this book. Poetry uses special language and is presented, not in sentences and paragraphs, but in lines and stanzas. In this way prosaic has come to mean *ordinary*.

250. An infirmity is a *disability* or *illness*. It refers to a weak condition of mind or body. If you suffer from one, you may need to spend some time in an infirmary.

BRAIN TICKLER
Set #66

Words in Context

Choose the correct list word (intricate, interlude, impart, prosaic, and infirmity) to complete the following sentences. Remember that the form of the word may differ slightly. Look for context clues.

Around forty years ago, it was not at all unusual for doctors to come to the homes of patients—even if the (1) _____ was only as (2) _____ as a sore throat. The procedure for arranging for a "house call" was not (3) _____. One only had to call, (4) _____ a brief description of the symptoms, and the doctor would arrive, more or less punctually. Naturally, the time between the phone call and the doctor's arrival might vary, since the doctor might fill that (5) _____ with visits to the homes of other patients. But who could complain? Imagine that kind of service nowadays.

(Answers are on page 227.)

Meet Words 251 to 255!

251. Arduous comes from the Latin word for "steep," and that makes sense, because arduous means very *difficult* to do. You may think that a life without lots of cable channels and video games would be arduous.

252. Premise comes from the Latin word *praemissus*, which means "to send before." A premise is a statement or fact that serves as the *basis* or *foundation* for whatever follows. For example, a boy who is afraid of line drives may not furnish much of a premise for an entire novel. (The plural form, premises, refers to a piece of real estate: Keep your dog off the premises, please!)

253. A book about baseball will not captivate, or *charm*, every reader because people have different tastes. Originally, the word meant to take captive, as one might capture a prisoner, but now it means to grab someone's attention or affection with charm, beauty, wit, and so on.

254. No one goes looking for adversity—*misfortune* or *danger*—but how a person responds to adversity reveals a great deal about that person's character. The word shares the same root as "adversary" (opponent) and "versus" (against).

255. Irony is a useful word to know. There are several kinds of irony worth noting. Verbal irony is the same thing as *sarcasm*, saying the opposite of what you mean. If you say, "That meal really looks delicious" when you know you wouldn't touch it with a ten-foot pole, you're using verbal irony. Situational irony occurs when the *unexpected* takes place. In the opening passage, the narrator identifies with the courageous third baseman, but as a lefty he could never play third base.

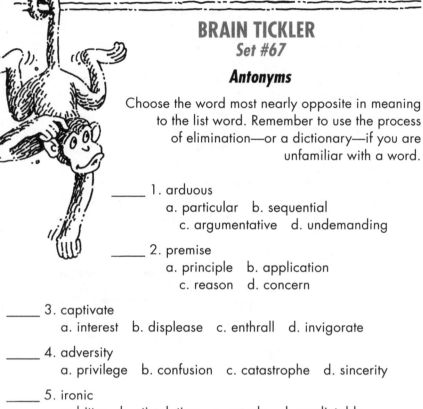

BRAIN TICKLER
Set #67

Antonyms

Choose the word most nearly opposite in meaning to the list word. Remember to use the process of elimination—or a dictionary—if you are unfamiliar with a word.

_____ 1. arduous
   a. particular   b. sequential
      c. argumentative   d. undemanding

_____ 2. premise
   a. principle   b. application
      c. reason   d. concern

_____ 3. captivate
   a. interest   b. displease   c. enthrall   d. invigorate

_____ 4. adversity
   a. privilege   b. confusion   c. catastrophe   d. sincerity

_____ 5. ironic
   a. bitter   b. stimulating   c. moody   d. predictable

(Answers are on page 227.)

BASEBALL'S NOT THE ONLY GAME IN TOWN

Word games abound, and many of them are easy to access and lots of fun. You might elect to go out and spend some money on purchasing some version of these games, but most of them can be found in your daily paper, in many magazines, and online. You can't be sure that each and every one will improve your vocabulary. Some, however, will do just that, and all will likely provide a pleasant diversion.

Here are just a few:

- Do you know what an anagram is? Well, here is an anagram of "anagram": manarag. Lots of word games employ this device, including Scramble, which appears in many newspapers.
- Word Searches will not force you to learn any new vocabulary words—you only have to locate them among a grid of letters—but they certainly will help you pass the time . . . that is, until eye strain sets in!
- It's not exactly a game, but Word of the Day calendars can be enjoyable and educational.
- Some TV shows have an educational orientation—*Jeopardy* and *Wheel of Fortune* are two that come immediately to mind—and watching them will certainly expose you to new words and terms.
- Are you a Scrabble fan? This board game has been around for many, many years, and its popularity has not waned one bit. Only through Scrabble will you learn that not every word that  begins with "q" has "u" as its second letter. In the process you may learn the meanings of such words as "qat" or "qiviut." In addition to the standard board game, you can purchase mini-games for car and plane trips, as well as a CD-ROM for computer use. For true Scrabble lovers, you must have the *Official Scrabble Players Dictionary*, which will very nicely complement your standard dictionary.
- That brings us to the grand master of word games, the crossword puzzle. You can learn a lot of new vocabulary words by doing crosswords, and the good thing is that you can very easily find puzzles that fit your ability level. Not only that, you can also find specialized puzzles that conform to your interests. Lots of magazines feature crossword puzzles whose themes appeal to the magazine's readers.

BRAIN TICKLER
Set #68

Words in Context

Choose the correct list word to complete the following sentences. Remember that the form of the word may differ slightly. Look for context clues. The list words are: avid, monopoly, myriad, nimble, devise, intricate, interlude, impart, prosaic, infirmity, arduous, premise, captivate, adversity, and irony.

1. The _____ wide receiver caught the ball, tiptoed along the sideline, and found his way into the end zone.

2. Tammy thinks she has a(n) _____ on ideas for fun things to do; whenever someone else comes up with a plan, she insists hers is better.

3. At one time, "fast foods" must have seemed like a strange _____ for a business, but these days it looks like a very profitable idea.

4. There's an uncomfortable _____ between the moment my brother asks my father for the car and the moment my father gives his answer.

5. If you keep at it long enough, you will certainly _____ a method to solve the problem.

6. One _____ after another sapped Jim's physical strength and stripped him of his will to live.

7. Sarah is a(n) _____ chef; she reads as much as she can about food, and she's always experimenting with new dishes and unusual recipes.

8. The _____ of the situation is that Jeremy had his first accident just one day after receiving a safe driver award.

9. If you have the money and an adventurous spirit, you'll find there are _____ places you can spend a wonderful vacation.

10. She is a magnificent performer, who never fails to _____ an audience.

11. Before she retired from a long, successful career with the firm, Sandy thought she would _____ some advice to younger employees on how to get along and get ahead.

12. Shakespeare's Hamlet did not count on having to deal with _____, and it took him a long while to confront his troubles head-on.

13. The last section of the Boston Marathon is particularly _____ because of an extended uphill section that tests even the best runners.

14. Not every problem demands a(n) _____ solution; in fact, sometimes the answer can be simple and obvious.

15. The teacher encouraged James to use a thesaurus in order to find interesting words to replace the _____ ones that too often characterized his writing.

(Answers are on page 227.)

ON YOUR OWN

Looking Ahead . . . and Behind

One day, when you're middle-aged and have teenage children of your own, you may impart to your children certain aspects of your own teen years. As your children listen to your tales, their respect for you may grow incrementally, as they learn the details of your arduous life. What will you say to your children about the life you currently enjoy? Use at least five words from this chapter.

THE LAST WORD

Have you ever read the famous short story, "The Necklace," by Guy de Maupassant? In this story, a young, beautiful woman of the working class attends a glamorous ball, but when she leaves this much-anticipated event, she loses the diamond necklace that she has borrowed from her wealthy friend. She and her husband borrow a great deal of money to replace the necklace, then spend the next ten years working like dogs to repay all the loans. In doing so, this proud young woman loses not only her youth, but also her most prized possession, her beauty. At the end of the story, she again meets her wealthy friend and proudly discloses the truth—that the necklace was lost, a replacement was obtained, and the friend never noticed the difference. Her friend, horrified, tells her that the diamonds were false. False. Bogus. Paste. Now that's irony, right?

BRAIN TICKLERS—THE ANSWERS

Set #65, page 219

1. monopoly
2. devise
3. nimble
4. myriad
5. avid

Set #66, page 221

1. infirmity
2. prosaic
3. intricate
4. impart
5. interlude

Set #67, page 223

1. d
2. b
3. b
4. a
5. d

Set #68, page 225

1. nimble
2. monopoly
3. premise
4. interlude
5. devise
6. infirmity
7. avid
8. irony
9. myriad
10. captivate
11. impart
12. adversity
13. arduous
14. intricate
15. prosaic

CHAPTER EIGHTEEN

Dare to "Dis"– Bullying the Bullies

Electronic Readers

A seventh grade boy walks down the hall, hurrying to his next class. He turns the corner and heads for the staircase, and slams into a trio of larger, older boys.

"Yo, dork. Where you going?"

"Loser, you trying to start something with my friend here?"

The most malicious of the three grabs the boy's shirt and stares into his eyes for five painfully long seconds. Then the three thugs break into spontaneous laughter.

The ordeal is over, for now.

If you inquire about the major social problem in middle schools, the one most students are likely to name is bullying. Students know this, teachers know this, and administrators know it, too, but in many cases, no matter how the school community perseveres, no one seems to be able to eliminate the problem.

Why is bullying so prevalent in middle schools? Are teachers so oblivious as to overlook situations right under their noses? Are administrators completely indifferent to the plight of innocent victims?

Several factors contribute to the perplexing nature of this problem. One is that almost all incidents occur beyond the reach of adults—in the unstructured, unsupervised situations that arise in hallways, stairwells, locker rooms, and so forth. A second explanation is that most victims are simply not inclined to report incidents to the authorities. They believe that "ratting out" a bully will only lead to more and worse bullying, and they are skeptical of school officials' ability to address the problem. And who can blame them for feeling despondent? Has bullying ever seemed like a recent phenomenon? Has anyone ever heard of a school or community without bullies? No, it's been going on forever and everywhere.

One teacher, Ms. Nancy Gunning, has an innovative solution: Teach kids how to stand up to bullies—teach kids how to use their wits to put bullies at a disadvantage. Very rarely does bullying result in real violence, she believes, because then a physical incident would have to come to the attention of the authorities, and the bullies don't want that to happen.

There's a delicate art to "dissing," and learning to "dis" effectively requires a great deal of tact. A weak dis will be completely ineffective, while an overly aggressive one will only raise the conflict. A potential victim needs to master that middle ground of dissing. He must use his wits to unhinge his opponent, to leave him momentarily confused, while he makes his own escape, his dignity intact. Ms. Gunning believes that these skills can be taught and learned. Bullies, after all, will always exist, but they needn't have their way.

Meet Words 256 to 260!

256. Malicious is the adjective form of the noun "malice," which means ill will or a desire to hurt others. The malicious bully is the one with the worst intentions, the one most likely to do harm. The root *mal* usually means "bad." For example, "malaria" literally means "bad air."

257. A spontaneous act or event is one that just happens; it isn't planned or prearranged. In the passage above, laughter occurs spontaneously. (It usually does, right?)

258. Long ago, an ordeal was a bizarre, unfair kind of trial, which worked like this: a person was exposed to great physical dangers, and only by surviving these dangers could he prove himself innocent. Now it refers to any kind of difficult or trying experience, such as dealing with a trio of bullies.

259. To inquire is to *ask*. You may be familiar with the noun form, "inquiry," which can mean either a single question or an entire investigation.

260. To persevere is to keep at something, in spite of its difficulty. Often one must persevere in order to achieve success at challenging tasks, such as finding a response to the problem of school bullying.

BRAIN TICKLER
Set #69

Nuts or Not?

Read each sentence to decide if the underlined vocabulary word is used correctly in context. If the meaning is ludicrous, write "Nuts" in the blank space. If the sentence makes sense, write "Not" in the blank space.

_____ 1. My new Spanish teacher seems to be so <u>malicious</u>! She gave us a homework assignment, but when everybody complained about the upcoming test in science, she delayed its due date.

_____ 2. "I can't help it if I'm always calling out," Randi explained to her teacher. "It's just that I'm <u>spontaneous</u> by nature."

_____ 3. Have you ever run a marathon? I'm in good shape, but I'm not sure I could stand that kind of an <u>ordeal</u>.

_____ 4. The waiter finally came over to our table, gave us the menus, and <u>inquired</u> about the evening's specials.

_____ 5. Jacqueline has a lot of talent in science, but she always <u>perseveres</u> in her labs and ends up receiving awful grades.

(Answers are on page 241.)

Meet Words 261 to 265!

261. When we say that bullying is prevalent in middle school, we mean that it's *widespread*. It's happening everywhere! (The verb form, "prevail," has a similar meaning—to become widespread—but it also means to be triumphant: usually the better team prevails.)

262. A person who is oblivious fails to notice or to remember. If you are not paying attention, your teacher may wonder if your daydreaming has brought you to the threshold of oblivion.

263. School administrators are certainly not indifferent to the problem of bullying! On the contrary, they care a great deal about this problem and wish they could figure out a way to solve it.

264. Plight comes from the Middle English *plit*, which means a *state* or *condition*, especially a dangerous or embarrassing one. (If you see words with that -ght base, you can assume they come from Middle English and Germanic words.)

265. How to deal with bullying? That's a perplexing problem, all right, because it's very hard to figure out, very *confusing*. What subject matter perplexes you? (There's the verb form for you.)

BRAIN TICKLER
Set #70

Synonyms

Match the list word with the word closest in meaning. Remember that there are two ways to deal with words whose meanings you don't know. One is to use the process of elimination; the other is to find a dictionary.

1. _____ prevalent
   a. certain   b. concrete   c. dilapidated
   d. common

2. _____ oblivious
   a. concerned   b. insensible   c. luxurious   d. pleasing

3. _____ indifferent
   a. involved   b. unconcerned   c. zealous   d. engaged

4. _____ plight
   a. situation   b. security   c. response   d. deliberation

5. _____ perplexing
   a. puzzling   b. humorous   c. provocative   d. accidental

(Answers are on page 241.)

Meet Words 266 to 270!

266. Inclined is the past participle form of the verb "incline." As it is used in the chapter's opening passage, it means *liable* or *willing*. But, as a verb, "incline" can also mean to place on a slope; from math, you might be familiar with an inclined plane.

267. When you feel despondent about something, you've pretty much given up hope and courage. That's exactly how bullies' victims feel when no one seems capable of addressing their plight.

268. A phenomenon is an *event, circumstance,* or *fact* that is apparent to the senses. (Its plural form is "phenomena.") Sometimes the word has a slightly different connotation and refers to a highly unusual event. In its adjective form, "phenomenal," it takes on a very positive connotation and means "remarkable."

269. Already you've come across the word "novelty," which means something new and original. The adjective form of this word is "novel." Innovative means just about the same thing: *new, inventive,* even *ground-breaking.* The suggestion that schools teach victims how to bully the bullies is innovative, indeed, because it is new and unusual.

270. If you possess a degree of tact, you can go very far in this world. Have you ever heard the expression, "a bull in a china shop"? Well, that's the exact opposite of tact. "Tact" refers to a sense of knowing the right thing to say or do in a situation without hurting anyone's feelings. If a former victim is planning on turning the tables on someone who has bullied him, he'd better exercise some tact.

BRAIN TICKLER
Set #71
Verbal Analogies

Select the list word (inclined, despondent, phenomenon, innovative, tact) that completes each analogy. Remember the importance of using a "bridge" in solving verbal analogies: create a sentence that clearly describes the relationship between the given pair. Consider the following problem:

oblivious : alert :: blunt : _____

Examining the given pair, you might produce a bridge that reads like this: "Oblivious is the opposite of alert." Having done so, you would look to find a word that creates the same relationship in the second pair. In this case, you'd be looking for an antonym of "blunt." ("Tactful" would do the trick.)

Bear in mind, though, that the bridge is not always so obvious.

Let's say the given pair was: diplomat : tact. In this case, you might produce this bridge: "A diplomat is someone who relies on tact." Apply these guidelines to the analogies that follow.

1. victory : joyful :: tragedy : _____

2. diplomacy : _____ :: spontaneous : unplanned

3. _____ : disinterested :: oblivious : attentive

4. occurrence : _____ :: ordeal : trial

5. diamond : costly :: modernization : _____

(Answers are on page 241.)

ELECTRONIC READERS

In the middle of the fifteenth century, a German gold-smith by the name of Johannes Gutenberg invented a printing press, which revolutionized the whole business of printing. Now, a Gutenberg press could print over 3,000 pages a day. The publishing industry was off to a flying start.

That was less than 500 years ago. In the first quarter of the twenty-first century, the invention of the electronic reader may make hardcover and paperback books obsolete.

Several factors account for the escalating popularity of electronic readers. First of all, they are very convenient. A reader weighs less than a hardcover book, and it can fit easily into a coat pocket or a briefcase. One electronic reader can contain hundreds of titles; thus, an avid reader can carry his own personal library wherever he goes. Moreover, electronic readers are environmentally friendly; trees don't have to die for books to live. Finally, electronic readers make sense economically. The cost of purchasing a bestselling e-book is considerably less than the cost of purchasing its hardcover counterpart.

So, for these reasons, it's quite possible that the next generation will read even more than twentieth-century folks did. And for that reason alone, they may grow impressive vocabularies.

And electronic readers contain another feature that will certainly aid vocabulary development. They contain built-in dictionaries. All you need to do is bring the cursor to a word, tap on it, and a definition will appear. It's ridiculously easy to deal with new vocabulary words, and, consequently, watching your vocabulary grow is, well, simply painless.

But before you rush out and buy one, do some home-work. Electronic readers are still relatively new, so their features—and prices—are changing all the time.

BRAIN TICKLER
Set #72

Words in Context

Choose the correct list word to complete the following sentences. Remember that the form of the word may differ slightly. Look for context clues. The list words are: malicious, spontaneous, ordeal, inquire, persevere, prevalent, oblivious, indifferent, plight, perplexing, inclined, despondent, phenomenon, innovative, and tact.

1. A car accident can be a terrible _____, especially if someone is injured.

2. "I am looking for a summer job," Hank said, "and I'd like to _____ about the possibility of a position."

3. Karen felt that her embarrassing situation was unique and that none of her friends had ever experienced a(n) _____ similar to hers.

4. After their dog ran away, the Garretts felt _____ for weeks.

5. It's best to use some _____ when you tell the boss you'll be taking a couple of weeks of vacation in the middle of August.

6. Greg was critical of the older bullies, yet he was completely _____ to the fact that he himself sometimes bullied smaller boys.

7. The ancient Greeks invented myths to explain certain natural _____, such as earthquakes and rain.

8. Marisa was not fleet or strong, but she _____, and eventually she won a starting spot on the lacrosse team.

9. After a big meal, I am not _____ to order a rich dessert. Something light, like fruit, works much better for me.

10. It's hard for most people to see crimes against victims as anything other than _____ acts.

11. The Smiths' new blender was equipped with several pleasing _____, including a device for crushing ice cubes.

12. "Why can't we just make a(n) _____ decision?" Max asked. "Why do we have to sort through the pros and cons of every single option?"

13. If a student takes a long time to get started on an assignment, chances are he finds the task _____.

14. In the Northeast, thunderstorms are _____ during the summer. Sometimes they actually come in bunches.

15. I am _____ as to the specific location of our summer vacation. I only care about getting away and taking it easy.

(Answers are on page 241.)

ON YOUR OWN

Is bullying a problem in your school? How does your school deal with it? Do you think this approach is effective? What additional recommendations would you suggest? Answer in a good body paragraph, one that has a good topic sentence and at least five supporting sentences—and, as always, use at least five list words from this chapter. (If you feel that bullying is not a major problem in your school, feel free to focus on your school's handling of another problem.)

THE LAST WORD

Way, way back in the 1960s, young people coined a word that meant just about the same thing as "cool" or splendid. That word was "groovy." (Yes, really.) Among the younger set, "groovy" became the word of choice to describe someone's bellbottoms or one's weekend plans or the latest hit from the Beatles or . . . anything! Its use spread like wildfire. Before long, it was heard in songs and on television and eventually (perish the thought!) from the mouths of thirty-somethings. What soon happened was that it became un-groovy to say "groovy."

Do you ever hear the word being used today? Not very often.

The word "dis" came into being in much the same way. It will be interesting to see whether it follows the same arc as its groovy predecessor.

BRAIN TICKLERS—THE ANSWERS

Set #69, page 233

1. nuts
2. not
3. not
4. nuts
5. nuts

Set #70, page 235

1. d
2. b
3. b
4. a
5. a

Set #71, page 237

1. despondent
2. tact
3. inclined
4. phenomenon
5. innovative

Set #72, page 239

1. ordeal
2. inquire
3. plight
4. despondent
5. tact
6. oblivious
7. phenomena
8. persevered
9. inclined
10. malicious
11. innovations
12. spontaneous
13. perplexing
14. prevalent
15. indifferent

CHAPTER NINETEEN

We're Smarter Than You Are—The Younger Generation Makes Its Case

Using the Context: A Case Study

What does it mean to be smart? Everyone knows people who earn high grades in school and on standardized tests. These people are generally considered intelligent. However, with this sort of intelligence comes an unflattering stereotype. It's the stereotype of the school-smart person who lacks another kind of intelligence—common sense, or "street smarts." It's the stereotype of the person who, despite his or her book smarts, lacks sophistication.

Certain tests, like the SAT exam you'll be taking in a few years, reduce the concept of academic aptitude to verbal (language) and mathematics ability. However, most experts in the field of intelligence have come to the conclusion that intelligence is a versatile concept. It is flexible enough to include the conventional kinds of intelligence (those measured by the SAT), as well as some categories of ability that once would not have been considered intelligence. These include musical intelligence, spatial intelligence (including art, engineering, and manual ability), and athletic intelligence.

Theories of multiple intelligence also include two kinds of social intelligence. Do you have a classmate to whom people turn when they have a problem? Do you know someone who seems especially competent at helping a group of people complete a task? Well, isn't it fair that intelligence theories recognize as "smart" the nation's future problem-solvers and leaders?

But here's a strange fact: IQ scores have been rising. Yes, we're actually getting smarter. A writer, Steven Johnson, recently conjectured that two factors responsible for this increase are television and video games, long considered the chief culprits for poor school performance and just about everything else that ails our society.

How do video games make you smarter? Well, there's the obvious benefit of improved hand-eye coordination, but that's not the most important factor. Johnson claims that today's video games are incredibly demanding. Often, the rules of the game are ambiguous, and it can take a long time for a new player to figure them out. Then, making on-the-spot decisions can be equally confusing because the options are vague and their outcomes are uncertain. Today's video games, which can last for as long as forty hours, are a lot harder than a game of checkers!

And television? How can television possibly make you smarter? Johnson argues that today's TV shows are much more complicated than those of a previous generation. Making sense of a show like *Lost* or *Law and Order* demands concentration. It asks the viewer to use what he or she knows about human nature to reach conclusions about the characters' personalities and motivations. And the plots of today's TV shows twist and turn in ways they never did before. You may not need an advanced degree to watch network TV, but you certainly have to think.

So, the next time your mom implores you to shut the TV or quit that video game and do your schoolwork, simply explain to her that these activities may increase your intelligence more than reading a few pages in your history text and answering a couple of comprehension questions.

Meet Words 271 to 275!

271. If you strip "unflattering" (which means "unfavorable") of its prefix and suffix, you are left with flatter. The word comes from the Middle English *flateren*, which means "to smooth" or "to touch gently." From this, it's not hard to see how "flatter" got its present meaning: to *praise* excessively or insincerely, usually to gain another's favor. The noun form of the word is "flattery."

272. A stereotype is a commonly held belief about a particular group of people. When we label people with an overly general statement that applies to some but not to all, we create stereotypes. "Stereotype" can also be used as a verb.

273. Sophistication is not an easy quality to describe. A sophisticated person is *worldly* in terms of knowledge, manners, and culture. A sophisticated reader is someone who is

perceptive enough to understand the subtleties of the printed word. Sophisticated equipment is modern, specialized, and advanced.

274. Aptitude is *ability* or *talent*. The SAT (Scholastic Aptitude Test) claims to measure one's ability to succeed academically.

275. To be versatile is to be capable in many areas. We say a baseball player is versatile if that player can handle several positions. Intelligence is a versatile concept because it can encompass many different skills.

BRAIN TICKLER
Set #73

Extremes

Think about words that suggest extremes. Would you rather see an interesting movie or a riveting one? Each of the following sentences contains a list word (or a form of it) and one paired with it. One suggests an extreme; one does not. Circle the word that best fits the sentence.

1. He asked me if I liked his speech. "It was wonderful," I replied, "and I hope you know this is honest praise/flattery."

2. It would be a mistake to characterize/stereotype Marilyn Monroe as a "dumb blonde," because in reality she was a remarkably gifted comedic actress.

3. Isaac possesses the kind of knowledge/sophistication you would expect of someone who has attended excellent schools, traveled extensively, and immersed himself in the world of the arts.

4. Eric Clapton can play so many notes so quickly and so beautifully that there can be no denying his aptitude/genius on the guitar.

5. "This garment," the salesman explained, "is extremely versatile/useful. You can wear it in any season and for practically any occasion."

(Answers are on page 256.)

Meet Words 276 to 280!

276. A convention is an agreement between persons about the practices of social life. Therefore, that which is conventional conforms to agreed-upon standards. It is *predictable*, *safe*, even *conservative*. The SAT measures conventional kinds of intelligence.

277. You are certainly familiar with the noun form of "manual," a book or booklet that provides directions or guidance. As an adjective, manual refers to that which is done with the hands. (It comes from the Latin and Middle English words for "hand.") A carpenter, for example, displays considerable manual aptitude.

278. To be competent is to be *capable* or *qualified*. You would rather hire a competent attorney than an incompetent one, right?

279. Conjecture is another word with Latin and Middle English roots: *conjectus* means to throw or bring together. In this case, ideas or evidence are thrown together, and the result means just about the same as *prediction* or *guesswork*. In the introductory passage, it's used as a verb, meaning to *guess* or to *theorize*.

280. A culprit is a person who is either accused or found guilty of a crime. In the opening passage, TV and video games— not exactly people—are the culprits, which shows that the definition has broadened somewhat.

BRAIN TICKLER
Set #74

Descriptions Inferred from Action

Choose the vocabulary word (conventional, manual, competent, conjecture, culprit) that describes the person, animal, or thing that would do the action mentioned. Write that word in the blank.

1. _____ You would commit a crime and leave behind just enough evidence to get caught.

2. _____ Whatever you do, you seem to do well.

3. _____ You don't mind formulating a theory that just might explain a confusing event.

4. _____ You can take apart an automobile engine, and you can put one back together.

5. _____ You don't like to stray too far from normal.

(Answers are on page 256.)

Meet Words 281 to 285!

281. Coordination is the process of making two or more things work together. To play video games well, you have to coordinate the movements of your eyes and hands.

282. The word ambiguous is used to denote *uncertain* meaning. What makes today's video games so hard to play is the fact that the rules are ambiguous.

283. An option is a *choice* or an *alternative*.

284. Vague has two related meanings. One is similar to the meaning of "ambiguous": *unclear*. You can say that the game's directions were vague and therefore hard to understand. Another meaning is *hazy* or *indistinct*.

285. To implore is to *ask* for help. Implore is a transitive verb, which means that it always gets a direct object, and that direct object is always a person. For example, you may implore your father to give you a lift into town.

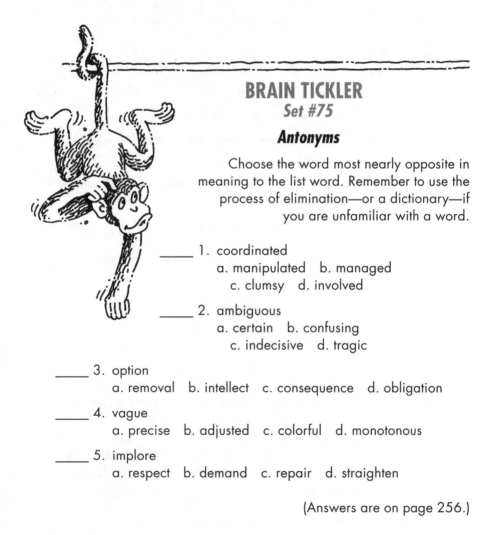

BRAIN TICKLER
Set #75

Antonyms

Choose the word most nearly opposite in meaning to the list word. Remember to use the process of elimination—or a dictionary—if you are unfamiliar with a word.

_____ 1. coordinated
   a. manipulated   b. managed
   c. clumsy   d. involved

_____ 2. ambiguous
   a. certain   b. confusing
   c. indecisive   d. tragic

_____ 3. option
   a. removal   b. intellect   c. consequence   d. obligation

_____ 4. vague
   a. precise   b. adjusted   c. colorful   d. monotonous

_____ 5. implore
   a. respect   b. demand   c. repair   d. straighten

(Answers are on page 256.)

USING THE CONTEXT:
A CASE STUDY

It's a good idea to read for fun. While you're reading for fun, it's also a good idea to take on some challenging material, but you won't get a lot out of material that's too challenging. Reading experts think that, in terms of words whose meanings you don't know, about one per page is challenging enough. Once you go beyond that, you're probably looking at material that is too difficult for you.

Let's take a look at this opening passage from Jane Austen's novel, *Emma*, and see if it's too difficult for you:

> Emma Woodhouse, handsome, clever, and rich, with a comfortable home and happy <u>disposition</u>, seemed to unite some of the best blessings of existence, and had lived nearly twenty-one years in the world with little to distress or <u>vex</u> her.
>
> She was the youngest of the two daughters of a most affectionate, <u>indulgent</u> father, and had, in consequence of her sister's marriage, been <u>mistress</u> of his house from a very early period. Her mother had died too long ago. . . .

First of all, we have to concede that Jane Austen's language and style (early nineteenth century) will test most contemporary readers. However, knowing what you do about using the context, you may discover that this passage is not as difficult as it might first seem.

Four words might challenge you:

- "Disposition" could be trickiest of the bunch, but it's also the one you're most likely to know. You have probably heard someone say that someone else has a lovely (or lousy) disposition, and you've probably interpreted this to mean "nature" or "personality." But, even if you didn't, you could still reach that same conclusion, just by using the process of elimination. You already know that Emma is "handsome, clever, and rich" and that she lives in a "comfortable home." What else, after all, does someone need? A "happy disposition," Austen would—and did—say.
- "Vex" is easy because it's paired with "distress" and means just about the same thing.
- You can figure out "indulgent" in the same way. Her father is "affectionate" and "indulgent." The first you already know, so you might be able to conclude from this and other information that Mr. Woodhouse has spoiled Emma. Indeed, he has. "Indulgent" means lenient or understanding.
- You might already know one meaning of "mistress" (an unflattering one), but another, somewhat outdated one is intended here. Again, you can use evidence from the passage to figure it out. A direct consequence of Emma's sister's marriage is that Emma has become the mistress, or woman-in-charge, of the house. Her mother would normally have held this position, but the last sentence tells you why she does not.

So using the context is a little like detective work. Are you ready for *Pride and Prejudice*?

BRAIN TICKLER
Set #76

Words in Context

Choose the correct list word to complete the following sentences. Remember that the form of the word may differ slightly. Look for context clues. The list words are: flatter, stereotype, sophistication, aptitude, versatile, conventional, manual, competent, conjecture, culprit, coordination, ambiguous, options, vague, and implore.

1. Ms. Stein told Randi that portions of her creative writing piece were _____, and she suggested she use vivid images to give the work a sense of clarity.

2. James was delighted with his new, _____ bicycle, which could be used as a racer, a touring bike, or a dirt bike.

3. Brad liked to _____ his mom with compliments about her cooking, but she told him that his most sincere statement was his request for a second helping.

4. Because Phil was such a(n) _____ writer, Mr. Brandt asked him to help other students with their writing assignments.

5. Mark brought his parking ticket to court, hoping to prove with the photos he'd taken that the parking signs were impossibly _____.

6. Satire is a difficult genre for students to master, but Jenny seemed to display some _____ for that form of expression.

7. The substitute teacher _____ the class to be quiet and begin the assignment, but the youngsters ignored him.

8. My neighbor likes to think of people in terms of _____, instead of seeing members of different racial groups as individuals.

9. Juggling three balls at once requires considerable _____, much more than I actually possess.

10. The troops thought the enemy would use only primitive weapons and were therefore surprised to discover that the enemy possessed such _____ firepower.

11. The waiter told us of our dessert _____, one sounding better than the next.

12. Plumbing may be a(n) _____ trade, but a plumber has to be able to think quickly and make some hard decisions.

13. We decided to do away with the _____ seating card business and just let the guests sit where they wanted.

14. The district attorney pointed to the defendant and exclaimed to the court, "Yes, this man is the _____!"

15. In England the weather changes so often it's nearly pointless to _____ what conditions a given day may bring.

(Answers are on page 256.)

ON YOUR OWN

This chapter's introductory essay deals with the idea that something that is commonly thought to be bad for you can actually be good. Write a convincing body paragraph about something else that fits this description. (Or, if you like, you can go the other way: Write about something commonly thought to be good for you that's actually bad.)

Here's the trick, however. Instead of using five words from this chapter, get out your thesaurus and replace any five with five especially apt synonyms.

THE LAST WORD

Once you know the meaning of culprit, you can harbor a pretty good guess as to the meaning of a few other words. The key here is recognizing that the Latin word *culpa* means guilt. So if your parents tell you that, even though your kid sister broke the window, you are culpable, then you can sense they're telling you that you should have done a better job of watching her. In other words, they're not entertaining any arguments about your culpability. You might as well just admit, "Mea culpa," Latin for "my bad."

BRAIN TICKLERS—THE ANSWERS

Set #73, page 247

1. praise
2. stereotype
3. sophistication
4. genius
5. versatile

Set #74, page 249

1. culprit
2. competent
3. conjecture
4. manual
5. conventional

Set #75, page 250

1. c
2. a
3. d
4. a
5. b

Set #76, page 253

1. vague
2. versatile
3. flatter
4. competent
5. ambiguous
6. aptitude
7. implored
8. stereotypes
9. coordination
10. sophisticated
11. options
12. manual
13. conventional
14. culprit
15. conjecture

CHAPTER TWENTY

The Borrowed Child
Looking Back

In 1941, life was especially precarious for the Jews in and around the small Polish town of Novogrudek.

The Nazis had invaded Poland in 1939, so it was just a matter of time before their authority was fully felt in eastern Poland. It was not that long a wait. In 1941 the Jews of the area were herded into a ghetto in the town. Then the killings began. In December of 1941—in one day—the Nazis slaughtered more than 4,000 people at Novogrudek.

The three Bielski brothers quickly assessed their slim chances of surviving, gathered whatever and whomever they could, and headed for the protection of the forest. Under the custody of these brothers, more than 1,200 Jews would miraculously survive the war. They would be known as the Bielski Brigade.

One Jew who would have to survive the war in another fashion altogether was tiny Lola Dzienciolski, an infant when the exodus to the forest first got underway. The presence of an infant in the forest posed two problems. First, it was unlikely that such a young and vulnerable child could survive the bitter winters. Second, a crying infant could draw unwanted attention from German soldiers on the lookout for Jews in hiding.

Lola's parents, Abraham and Taiba, knew what they had to do: they had to place their baby with a non-Jewish family. Through a series of covert negotiations, the Bielski brothers found a childless couple, the Kenceivicas, who were willing to take the baby. To neutralize the inevitable suspicions of the couple's neighbors, late one night the Bielski brothers left the baby in a mound of snow right under the window of the Kenceivica home, and Mrs. Kenceivica pretended to find her there.

While her biological parents battled the elements and the Nazis, Lola Kenceivica grew up with her surrogate parents. As far as she knew, they were her only parents. They loved her as if she were their own; she returned their affection.

When the war ended in 1945 and the Jews of Novogrudek were free to leave the forest, Lola's parents came looking for her. However, the Kenceivicas were unwilling to relinquish their "daughter." So the biological parents, no strangers to desperate measures, seized the girl while she was briefly left unattended. Lola cried for her "parents" and begged these strange, disheveled people who had abducted her to return her to what she believed were her rightful mother and father. Later she would ask them to let her go to church.

It is nearly impossible to imagine the mental state of the forlorn Kenceivicas.

After spending more than a year in a displaced persons camp, Lola and her family would immigrate to the United States. She grew up in Brooklyn, New York, married, and raised a family in New Jersey, where she lives today.

In 1993, Lola Kline and some of her relatives organized a trip to Belarus (the town of Novogrudek had over the years "migrated" from Poland to Russia and now to Belarus) to try to recapture some of these memories from long ago and to see what had become of the area. There Lola located the house where she had lived with the Kenceivicas, and she met a man who remembered her from those days when she lived with her adopted parents.

This experience evoked powerful feelings in Lola. Who would not feel a sense of loss for what has been taken and cannot be returned? Who would not feel powerless about events that wartime imposes? Who would not feel wonder at life's unimaginably strange twists and turns?

Meet Words 286 to 290!

286. Precarious has two main meanings. The one used in this passage suggests danger and peril, words that would certainly describe the situation for the Jews in Novogrudek, with the Nazis on their doorstep. A second meaning is *unstable* or *risky*. You can say that the glass, placed at the very edge of the table, is in a precarious position.

287. You know that authority also has several meanings. It can refer to the *power* or the *right* to make decisions or take actions. It was only a matter of time before the Nazis would assert their authority in Novogrudek. Authority can also refer to a person's considerable *knowledge* on a particular subject. Finally, we refer to such a person as an authority.

288. Ghetto is a word whose meaning is changing. Originally, ghetto was used exactly as it appears in this passage: a section to which Jews were restricted. But it has come to mean any section of a city where people of a particular racial or ethnic group are confined. Very recently, the word has been used as a slang adjective to describe styles originating in the inner city.

289. To assess is to *consider, evaluate,* or *measure.* Sometimes the word is used generally, but at other times it is used in a quantitative sense. Local officials may assess your home in order to determine your real estate taxes.

290. Custody refers to the *care* or *supervision* given to a person in need of it. You can say that as a young child you crossed the street under the custody of the school crossing guard. When we say that someone has been taken into custody, it usually has another connotation, suggesting that person has been arrested.

BRAIN TICKLER
Set #77

Synonyms

Match the list word with the word closest in meaning. Remember that there are two ways to deal with words whose meanings you don't know. One is to use the process of elimination; the other is to find a dictionary.

1. _____ precarious
   a. earlier   b. stable
   c. perilous   d. long-winded

2. _____ authority
   a. influence   b. servant
      c. document   d. condition

3. _____ ghetto
   a. rural   b. mansion   c. duplex   d. slum

4. _____ assess
   a. enter   b. retrieve   c. judge   d. overlook

5. _____ custody
   a. protection   b. neglect   c. sympathy   d. consideration

(Answers are on page 270.)

Meet Words 291 to 295!

291. An exodus is a mass *departure*. The second book of the Old
Testament describes the departure of the Israelites from
Egypt. This book is named "Exodus."

292. Covert comes from the same root as "cover." It means
concealed or *hidden* or *secretive*. When the Bielski brothers
were trying to find a temporary home for Lola, they had to
manage this in covert fashion, since none of the non-Jews
of Novogrudek wanted to be seen conversing with them.

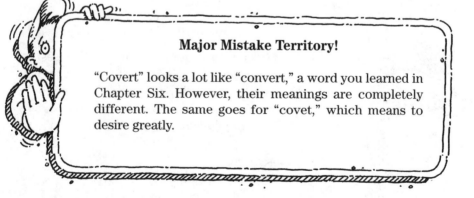

Major Mistake Territory!

"Covert" looks a lot like "convert," a word you learned in
Chapter Six. However, their meanings are completely
different. The same goes for "covet," which means to
desire greatly.

293. To negotiate is to discuss or bargain in order to reach an agreement. Negotiation is the name given to that process. Because the process often requires more than one attempt, the word is often expressed in plural form.

294. To neutralize is to *offset* or reduce the effect of some other force. The Bielski brothers, in order to neutralize suspicion, pretended to abandon the infant Lola. Neutralize can have a stronger meaning: It can mean to *paralyze* or *destroy*.

295. A surrogate is someone who substitutes for someone else. The Kenceivicas served as surrogate parents for Lola. You could say that a very effective, generous teacher or coach serves as a surrogate parent because that individual carries out some of the same responsibilities a parent does. Surrogate also has a specialized meaning. In the legal system, the surrogate courts take care of problems arising from wills and estates.

BRAIN TICKLER
Set #78

Descriptions Inferred from Action

Choose the vocabulary word (exodus, covert, negotiations, neutralize, surrogate) that describes the person, animal, or thing that would perform the action mentioned. Write that word in the blank.

1. _____ When Sean's father died, Sean, being the oldest child, tried to step up and assume some of his dad's responsibilities.

2. _____ During the emergency drill, the entire student body and faculty departed from the school and gathered across the road at the school's athletic fields.

3. _____ William knows he can counteract Tom's extremely aggressive chess playing only by playing a patient, defensive game and hoping that Tom blunders.

4. _____ In order to avoid a lockout or a strike, the players' union met with the owners until the wee hours of the morning.

5. _____ Plainclothes detectives can accumulate evidence against drug dealers by pretending to be customers interested in purchasing illegal drugs.

(Answers are on page 270.)

Meet Words 296 to 300!

296. To relinquish is to *give up*. (This is a great chance to consult your dictionary's pronunciation guide.) In order to save the child's life, as well as the lives of many in hiding, Abraham and Taiba had to relinquish their daughter.

297. Do you know that just-got-out-of-bed look? Well, sometimes a disheveled, or *messy*, look can be fashionable, but often it's not exactly a compliment. "Dishevel," the verb form, means to cause to become untidy.

298. Abduct is a painful word. To abduct someone is to capture that person by force. It comes from the Latin word *abducere*, which means "to lead away." The Bielskis had no choice but to abduct three-year-old Lola, because her surrogate parents would surely not have relinquished her willingly.

299. Forlorn comes from the Middle English verb "to lose completely." What makes you feel forlorn? Do you feel forlorn when your best friend moves to a different state? Do you feel somewhat forlorn when you come to the end of a great book? Do you feel forlorn when something you value dearly is lost or stolen?

300. To evoke is to *suggest* or *bring to mind*. For Lola, her trip to Belarus understandably evoked powerful feelings. The adjective form of the word, "evocative," means suggestive or moving.

BRAIN TICKLER
Set #79

Nuts or Not?

Read each sentence to decide if the underlined vocabulary word (or a form of it) is used correctly in context. If the meaning is ludicrous, write "Nuts" in the blank space. If the sentence makes sense, write "Not" in the blank space.

_____ 1. When I placed the tie and my credit card on the counter, I knew I had made up my mind to relinquish such an expensive item.

_____ 2. Joseph combed his hair, straightened his tie, and made his way downstairs for breakfast. "My," his mother remarked, "you look so disheveled this morning."

_____ 3. The enemy was not willing to release the prisoners, which left the commander no choice but to create a plan to abduct them.

_____ 4. When Mr. Bradford announced that she had scored the highest grade in the class, Megan could not keep a forlorn expression from appearing on her face.

_____ 5. The view of lower Manhattan's skyline always evokes sad memories of September 11, 2001.

(Answers are on page 270.)

LOOKING BACK

Do you know people who try unsuccessfully to lose weight and then keep that weight off? In some cases, that happens because they haven't gone far enough. Yes, they may have dieted successfully for a certain period of time, but permanent weight loss requires more than that. It requires enduring lifestyle changes—changing the way you eat and committing to a program of regular exercise.

The same is true of vocabulary growth. If you've read this book and learned most or all of the 300 featured vocabulary words, you've made a good start, but you haven't gone far enough. You need to make some lifestyle changes.

The sidebars in this book have provided you with ways to continue your vocabulary growth on your own. These are the most important ones:

- Become a more dedicated reader. Just as a determined dieter is not going to lose thirty pounds in a week, your growth as a reader must come in increments. Increase your reading time gradually. Start with material that very easily holds your attention; then read material that will require you to focus. Start with light, easy books and magazines; move on to more demanding material.
- Use the context. As you read and come across words you don't know, use the context of the passage to help you figure out the meanings of these words. You need to make a conscious effort to do this. Don't just gloss over words you don't know.

- Use that dictionary. Have you obtained a quality dictionary for yourself? Have you begun to use it regularly? Remember: This is not an occasion for you to save a few pennies. Spend the extra money on a really good dictionary. You'll use it for twenty-five years.
- Use that little black book. Do you remember that black book we talked about way back in Chapter Five? Have you purchased one yet? Where do you keep it? Is it with you most of the time? How many entries do you have? Remember: All the experts agree that you don't really acquire a word until you come across it three times.

BRAIN TICKLER
Set #80

Words in Context

Choose the correct list word to complete the following sentences. Remember that the form of the word may differ slightly. Look for context clues. The list words are: precarious, authority, ghetto, assess, custody, exodus, covert, negotiations, neutralize, surrogate, relinquish, disheveled, abduct, forlorn, and evoke.

1. For recent immigrants, _____ life has a major advantage: it offers a community consisting of people who speak the same language, eat the same foods, and observe the same customs.

2. After the touch football game, Brandon assured his parents that a shower and a set of clean clothes would repair his _____ appearance.

3. The military conducted a(n) _____ operation, which was not reported to the press or the general public.

4. The waiter told us eating some of the bread would _____ the hot, peppery spices in the meal.

5. Reading some of John Updike's Rabbit books will certainly _____ memories of the 1960s and 1970s.

6. Both William and Melissa wanted _____ of their children, and this became a contested matter in their divorce proceedings.

7. Ron found himself in a(n) _____ position: If he received one more speeding ticket, his driver's license would be suspended.

8. Recent acts of terrorism have involved the _____ of journalists, developers, and political figures.

9. Before you decide how much studying you need to do, why not take a few minutes to _____ what you already know?

10. Dana's mood turned _____ when she realized that her favorite stuffed animal had been lost.

11. Jessica has been working in the office for so long, she has become a(n) _____ mother to all the new employees.

12. I could never _____ my BlackBerry, because without it I wouldn't be able to stay on top of my hectic schedule.

13. When President Truman said, "The buck stops here," it was his way of acknowledging his _____ and his responsibility.

14. The ball game ended, and a(n) _____ of more than 50,000 fans began.

15. After several months of tense _____, both parties agreed to a contract.

(Answers are on page 270.)

ON YOUR OWN

Did you ever get knocked over by a wave?

We like to think that we're in control. That's a very comforting idea, actually. So maybe we cling to that idea partly because we know that there may come a time when the opposite is true, when our lives are swept up in events far greater than we are.

That would describe Lola Kline's early years.

Write a good body paragraph about someone you know whose life took an unpredictable turn because of factors beyond his or her control. These could be things like illnesses or war or natural disasters or family crises or . . . whatever.

In your body paragraph, be sure to use at least five list words from this chapter.

THE LAST WORD

Repeatedly we have examined degrees of meaning. In the English language, we have lots of words for sadness. Melancholy suggests a general mood of gloominess, a feeling of down-in-the-dumps. Despondent (Chapter 18) is a bit more painful, it seems. It comes from the Latin word *despondere*, which means to lose. But forlorn takes the cake, as its etymology ("to lose *utterly*") suggests.

BRAIN TICKLERS—THE ANSWERS

Set #77, page 261

1. c
2. a
3. d
4. c
5. a

Set #78, page 263

1. surrogate
2. exodus
3. neutralize
4. negotiations
5. covert

Set #79, page 265

1. nuts
2. nuts
3. not
4. nuts
5. not

Set #80, page 267

1. ghetto
2. disheveled
3. covert
4. neutralize
5. evoke
6. custody
7. precarious
8. abduction
9. assess
10. forlorn
11. surrogate
12. relinquish
13. authority
14. exodus
15. negotiations

APPENDIX

Word List—The words that appear in this book (chapters in parentheses)

A

abandon (2)
abate (1)
abduct (20)
abound (13)
abundance (7)
accelerate (7)
accumulate (15)
accustomed (2)
acknowledge (5)
acquire (6)
adjacent (7)
adopt (9)
adorn (1)
adversity (17)
advocate (16)
afflict (13)
agile (12)
allocate (10)
aloof (3)
altered (4)
amateur (14)
ambiguous (19)
amiable (15)
anticipate (4)
anxiety (16)
apparatus (6)
aptitude (19)
ardent (1)
arduous (17)
arrogance (2)
assert (13)
assess (20)
assimilate (9)
assure (11)

attire (5)
audible (14)
authentic (4)
authority (20)
avail (12)
avid (17)

B

benevolent (11)
brashly (11)
brawny (14)

C

caliber (9)
captivate (17)
catalyst (16)
cater (1)
cautious (9)
cite (16)
clench (2)
cliché (12)
competent (19)
complex (3)
comprehend (9)
comprise (7)
concede (6)
conception (4)
conclude (11)
condemn (16)
confine (16)
conform (5)
conjecture (19)
conscientious (9)
consume (10)

contemporary (7)
content (9)
conventional (19)
convert (6)
coordination (19)
covert (20)
critical (3)
crucial (15)
culprit (19)
curtail (16)
custody (20)
cynicism (14)

D

denounce (6)
dense (7)
derive (14)
descend (2)
despondent (18)
destitute (8)
deter (16)
deteriorate (15)
determine (3)
devastation (8)
devise (17)
devour (1)
diagnose (12)
dignity (15)
dilemma (10)
diminutive (5)
discard (10)
discern (9)

disclose (12)
discreetly (6)
disheveled (20)
dismayed (3)
distinct (10)
distraught (12)
dreary (2)
dwindle (11)

E

elated (15)
elicit (1)
elusive (13)
emaciated (13)
embark (12)
emerge (3)
enable (8)
encounter (6)
endure (1)
enhance (14)
ensue (12)
enthrall (1)
escalate (8)
essential (3)
establish (9)
evoke (20)
exert (5)
exodus (20)
extent (9)
extraordinary (1)

F

facilitate (16)
feign (10)

flatter (19)
flexible (8)
fluctuating (13)
foil (16)
forlorn (24)
former (1)
fragile (8)
fraudulent (14)
fundamental (13)
furtively (13)

G

ghetto (20)
glance (7)
gloat (2)
grueling (11)

H

humble (2)
humiliate (5)

I

images (7)
immune (12)
impart (17)
impede (13)
implore (19)
imposing (5)
inclined (18)
incremental (16)
incur (14)
indifferent (18)
industrious (10)
inevitable (8)
infer (11)
infirmity (17)
inflict (5)
inhabitable (8)
innovative (18)
inquire (18)
instill (2)

insufferable (6)
integrity (14)
interlude (17)
intimidate (5)
intimidating (15)
intricate (17)
intrude (6)
irony (17)

J

jeopardize (16)

L

lament (2)
legitimate (14)
leisurely (7)
liable (8)
limited (9)
literally (5)
loathe (3)

M

maintain (13)
malicious (18)
maneuver (7)
manifestation (13)
manual (19)
mass (4)
mentor (15)
merchant (10)
mingle (15)
miser (11)
modify (4)
monopoly (17)
monotonous (11)
morbid (12)
multitude (11)
mute (5)
mutter (10)

myriad (17)
myth (4)

N

naïve (4)
navigation (7)
negotiation (20)
neutralize (20)
nimble (17)
novelty (6)

O

obese (13)
oblivious (18)
obsessed (6)
obsolete (6)
offset (8)
ominous (9)
options (19)
optimistic (15)
ordeal (18)

P

paramount (9)
patron (10)
perceive (13)
peril (14)
perplexing (18)
persevere (18)
perspective (9)
peruse (7)
phenomenon (18)
plight (18)
policies (8)
ponder (1)
potential (10)
precarious (20)
predecessor (12)
predicament (15)

premise (17)
prevalent (18)
procrastinate (3)
procure (1)
promote (14)
prosaic (17)
provoke (5)
public (4)
pursuits (11)

Q

quest (10)

R

recurrence (12)
refrain (14)
regale (1)
relinquish (20)
reluctant (15)
remorse (7)
repel (13)
resolved (11)
restrict (13)
resume (11)
revise (3)

S

scour (12)
scrutinize (1)
seldom (3)
serenity (11)
sheer (1)
shrill (14)
significant (4)
simultaneously (6)
sinister (23)
skeptic (4)
smug (10)
soar (2)
solicitor (11)

sophistication (19)
speculate (4)
spontaneous (18)
succumb (5)
summon (3)
surrogate (20)
stability (7)
status quo (16)
stereotype (19)

subtle (10)
susceptible (8)
syndrome (15)
synthetic (14)
systems (8)

T

tact (18)
text (7)
threshold (15)

thrive (15)
tolerate (6)
typically (3)
tyrant (5)

U

uncouth (6)
unique (2)
upgrade (8)

V

vague (19)

vengeance (2)
versatile (19)
veteran (2)
vigorous (12)
vile (5)
vivid (8)
vulnerable (16)

W

wane (9)
whine (2)
wizardry (12)

Words from Greek and Roman Myths and Languages

These words owe their origins to Greek and Roman languages and myths. As you look up their definitions, be aware of the original meaning and the modern meaning.

1. Achilles' heel
2. Adonis
3. aegis
4. amazon
5. ambrosia
6. aphrodisiac
7. atlas
8. chronicle
9. crony
10. epidemic
11. gorgon
12. harpy
13. hectoring
14. hedonist
15. Herculean
16. hypnotic
17. iridescent
18. janitor
19. jovial
20. Junoesque
21. labyrinthine
22. laconic
23. lethargic
24. libation
25. lyric
26. marathon
27. martial
28. mentor
29. mercurial
30. metamorphosis
31. mnemonic
32. muse
33. narcissism
34. nectar
35. nemesis
36. odyssey
37. oracle
38. panacea
39. Pandora's box
40. pandemonium
41. panic
42. plutocrat
43. somnolent
44. sophomore
45. stoical
46. stygian
47. thespian
48. Trojan horse
49. utopian
50. zephyr

More Words to Know

The preface to this book explained to you that the selection of 300 new words in 20 chapters was somewhat random. The 270 words that follow are no less deserving than the original 300. Some of them are a bit more difficult; most are not. They are general words that teachers will often assume you already know. If you have been keeping a little black book, you will no doubt be familiar with some of them.

1. abstract	31. candidate	61. cultivate
2. accommodate	32. canvass (vb.)	62. debris
3. accomplice	33. capricious	63. debt
4. acquit	34. caress	64. deceive
5. acute	35. cease	65. decipher
6. adversary	36. censor	66. decline
7. affluent	37. chagrin	67. defile
8. agenda	38. charisma	68. deft
9. agitate	39. chide	69. delve
10. allege	40. clamber	70. demolish
11. ambivalence	41. cliques	71. deplore
12. amend	42. coarse	72. deprive
13. anonymous	43. coax	73. designate
14. appalling	44. commence	74. despair
15. appease	45. compel	75. detach
16. arbitrary	46. complacent	76. diffident
17. ardor	47. comply	77. din
18. assail	48. compromise	78. diplomatic
19. aspire	49. console	79. discriminate
20. audition	50. conspiracy	80. disdain
21. auspicious	51. consult	81. disperse
22. austere	52. contaminate	82. docile
23. belligerent	53. contempt	83. domestic
24. bewilder	54. contrive	84. drastic
25. bicker	55. converge	85. dreaded
26. bland	56. convey	86. dubious
27. bleak	57. corrupt	87. durable
28. blunt	58. counterfeit	88. dusky
29. boisterous	59. counterpart	89. earnest
30. brittle	60. covert	90. ebb

91. eccentric	133. hypocrite	175. perch
92. ecstasy	134. hypothesis	176. perpetual
93. elaborate	135. idiom	177. persist
94. elite	136. idle	178. philosophy
95. embroider	137. illusion	179. plausible
96. enchant	138. imminent	180. plunder
97. engrossed	139. impetuous	181. poise
98. epitome	140. improvise	182. pompous
99. ethnic	141. impulse	183. precede
100. evade	142. indignant	184. preside
101. exclude	143. indulge	185. primitive
102. exempt	144. insinuate	186. priority
103. exile	145. insolent	187. pristine
104. exotic	146. integrate	188. profess
105. expunge	147. intermittent	189. prophecy
106. faint (adj.)	148. interrogate	190. prudent
107. falter	149. intervene	191. pry
108. feeble	150. intimate	192. publicize
109. flaunt	151. inventory	193. pungent
110. folly	152. keen	194. radical
111. formidable	153. lavish	195. rapture
112. fray	154. linger	196. rash (adj.)
113. frugal	155. ludicrous	197. recede
114. fugitive	156. lure	198. reciprocate
115. futile	157. mandate	199. redeem
116. garrulous	158. martyr	200. reign
117. gaunt	159. meander	201. relevant
118. generalize	160. melancholy	202. relish (vb.)
119. glimmer	161. meticulous	203. reminisce
120. glossy	162. minute (adj.)	204. remnant
121. glum	163. moderate	205. reprimand
122. glutton	164. nostalgia	206. resigned
123. gratify	165. noteworthy	207. retaliate
124. grave (adj.)	166. nurture	208. reticent
125. grimy	167. oasis	209. retort
126. guile	168. obligated	210. revert
127. hasty	169. oblige	211. rigor
128. heir	170. obscure	212. robust
129. homogeneous	171. obsolete	213. rupture
130. honor	172. obstruction	214. ruthless
131. hover	173. passive	215. sanctuary
132. huddle (vb.)	174. peer (vb.)	216. scheme

217. scruples
218. sedate
219. segregated
220. seminar
221. shackle
222. sober
223. solitary
224. sparse
225. spite
226. squander
227. squat
228. stamina
229. stealth
230. subdue
231. submerge
232. subordinate
233. subside
234. suffice

235. sullen
236. taint
237. tarnish
238. taunt
239. tedious
240. tentative
241. tirade
242. trauma
243. tremor
244. trickle
245. trifle
246. trivial
247. tumult
248. turbulent
249. turmoil
250. ultimate
251. uproot
252. urgent

253. vapid
254. veil
255. venture
256. vigilant
257. vital
258. vocation
259. volition
260. waiver
261. wanton
262. warrant
263. wean
264. weary
265. whim
266. wholesome
267. wistful
268. withdraw
269. wither
270. yearn

INDEX

A

Accented syllables, 85
Anabolic steroids, 177–178
Analogy, verbal, 54, 63, 145, 196, 207, 237
Antonyms
  exercises involving, 5, 33, 81, 106, 132, 144, 156, 165, 179, 195, 223, 250
  in thesaurus, 119–120
"Anxious," 204
"Assert," 166

B

Black book, 68, 267

C

Case study, 251–252
"Cite," 208
"Content," 117
Context, words in, 6–9, 11–12, 26–27, 39–40, 51, 55–56, 69–70, 79, 83–84, 96–97, 105, 108–109, 121–122, 131, 134–135, 154–155, 158–159, 170–171, 181, 184–186, 193, 198–199, 211–213, 221, 225, 239–240, 253–254, 267–268
"Covert," 262
"Culprit," 255

D

Descriptions
  inferred from actions, 34, 77, 153, 205–206, 249, 263–264
  inferred from comments, 19, 65, 94, 129, 182–183, 219

"Devastation," 110
Dictionary
  description of, 81–83
  electronic, 107
  history of, 183–184
  online, 107
"Discreet," 76
"Discrete," 76

E

Electronic dictionaries, 107
Electronic readers, 238
Electronic thesaurus, 156–157
English dictionary, 183–184
English language, history of, 95
Etymology, 82
Exporting of words, 169–170
Extremes, 21, 67, 103, 247

H

Homonyms, 20, 76, 208

I

"Imply," 142
Importing of words, 169–170
"Infer," 142
"Instill," 28
Intelligence, 245
Introductory essay, 122

J

Johnson, Samuel, 184

L

"Literal," 64